Speaking Bipolar's 30 Days of Positivity

Positivity Club, Volume 1

Scott Ninneman

Published by Speaking Bipolar, 2024.

SPEAKING BIPOLAR'S 30 DAYS OF POSITIVITY

First edition. August 3, 2024.

ISBN: 979-8227987945

Written by Scott Ninneman.

Table of Contents

Special thanks to:

Jessie: Your love of reading inspired me to start writing again.

My mom: You endured the chaos of having a writer in your life.

Connie: Your encouragement helped me keep writing.

My readers: I keep writing because you keep showing up.

I love you all.

30 Days of Positivity

Welcome to Speaking Bipolar's 30 Days of Positivity!

Life in this world can be soul-crushing. Negativity flies at us from every direction, compounding and piling up until you can't breathe. Add on a mental illness and you suddenly feel like that camel with the broken back.

It doesn't have to be that way. To keep my balance, I try to focus on one positive thing every day. I'm going to help you do it, too.

My name is Scott Ninneman, and I'm the writer behind Speaking Bipolar. I received my bipolar disorder diagnosis in the spring of 1995. At first, I felt like my life was over, but then I learned to pick myself up and move forward. My journey is full of lots of trial and error, but in time, I discovered how to live a full life with bipolar disorder. I believe anyone can do the same, including you.

This book is part of how I've helped my readers live their best lives. It started a few years ago in the middle of fall. I noticed many comments on social media and from my readers about people fearing the holiday season. Every person doubted if they had enough strength to make it through the last weeks of the year. As I read the comments, I knew I had to help.

The 30 Days of Positivity email course was a lightbulb moment while sitting at my day job office desk. I decided I would write 30 simple posts, include links to similar content, and help everyone survive the end of the year.

The earliest readers loved the content, many asking for a book after they completed the 30 days. It's taken a while to get there, but this publication is a collection of those first 30 posts and the supporting stories.

Starting each day with a positive mindset can make your entire day better. This collection will help you change over the next 30 days.

Note: This book started as an online course. To continue the positivity after the 30 days, come join our family at the Speaking Bipolar Positivity Club[1].

Disclaimer: Scott Ninneman is not a mental health professional. The content of this book is based on his personal experiences and the tools he uses to manage his mental health. Nothing in this book should be taken as medical advice. If you are struggling with mental health issues, please seek professional help.

---

1. https://speakingbipolar.com/club

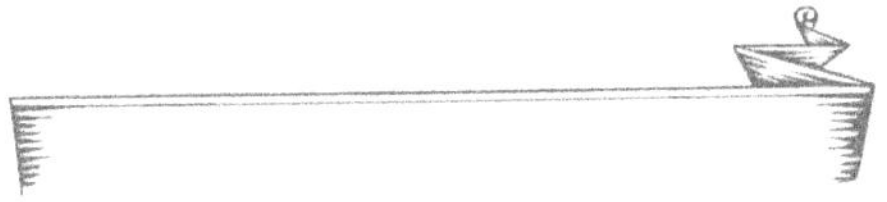

How To Use This Book

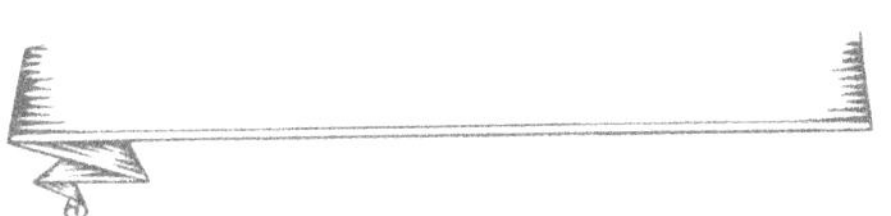

Each day has a lesson or a topic to focus on for the day. Included in each lesson are tips for reflecting on the day's theme. At the end of the lesson, there is a journal prompt and a creative writing prompt to inspire deeper thinking about the material. Then, after the lesson, is a chapter with more inspiration.

You may not be a writer and think you should skip the creative writing prompts, but spend some time with them, anyway. Put yourself in the place of the main character or use the text as a second journal prompt.

Added benefits to this book include:

- Understanding bipolar disorder better
- Learning to be more grateful
- Focusing on the better things in life

You'll also learn a little more about me along the way.

The goal of the 30 Days of Positivity books is to help you live your best life. If you take the time and do the work, you will reach the same levels of success my earliest readers found.

Are you ready to be more positive? Let's get started.

Day 1 | Approach Life With an Open Heart

Growing up in central Wisconsin during the 1970s, I lived by a set of internal rules. No one gave me a rulebook. Instead, every time I learned a lesson, I created a rule to live by.

Rule number one was to trust no one.

It was many years before I learned I had a mental illness while in my 20s. All I knew as a child was it was my job to keep me safe. This desire for safety led me to the habit of building walls around myself.

Think about your walls. No, not the four surrounding the room where you are reading this chapter. Instead, I mean your bipolar walls, the ones you build to protect yourself and others.

If you have bipolar disorder, you're likely skilled at building walls. You learned quickly how to put up barriers around your heart to keep yourself safe from the hurt that love can bring. But you may have also closed yourself off from the happiness and joy that friendships can offer.

It is only when you let go of your fears and open your heart completely that you can experience the true magic of love. While romantic love is wonderful, that's not the goal here. The best love often comes from friends who accept you for who you are and let you be yourself.

If you're afraid of getting hurt, remember that the only way to avoid pain is to never feel love. And what a sad life that would be.

The older I get, the more walls I can see around me. I've been building barriers for so long that I do it by instinct. The walls go up before I even think about them, but those boundaries distance me from people.

In the first months of the COVID-19 pandemic, I slipped into severe bipolar depression. During those painful months, I wondered why no one was checking on me. Where were my friends? Why didn't anyone see my pain?

Every day, I grew more angry and hurt. I was suffering, and no one cared.

Then I realized no one could see my suffering because I refused to show it. My walls had grown so thick that most of the people in my life no longer knew the real me. They knew the smile, the mask, the impenetrable wall. They knew the Scott I wanted them to know, and he never has bad days.

The only problem is he's not real. The only path for me to get the help I needed was to tear down some of my walls.

I started by reaching out to a few friends, just text messages at first, to say I needed help. I sent messages about how I was struggling and how hard the isolation felt. With each message, I removed my mask and revealed the pain I was fighting.

The outpouring of support was amazing, and much to my surprise, many of my friends felt the same way. Even those without bipolar disorder understood what I was feeling because the whole world felt scared and alone.

By taking the time to connect over our shared struggles, we grew closer, but it was only possible because I let others inside my walls.

Bipolar disorder can make it difficult to maintain close relationships. The fear of abandonment and rejection can make you build fences to protect your heart, making it harder for others to get close to you. So, it's essential to remember that love is worth the risk. Let others in so you can love and be loved in return.

Without friendship, life is empty. Even with the fear of being hurt, take a chance and allow someone into your heart. You might just find the love and happiness that you've been searching to find. And you deserve to be loved.

Journal Prompt: What walls have you built around your heart? How have they affected your relationships?

Creative Writing Prompt: Write a story about an old woman tearing down her walls. Where does she start? What happens as a result?

Listen for the Silent "I Love You's"

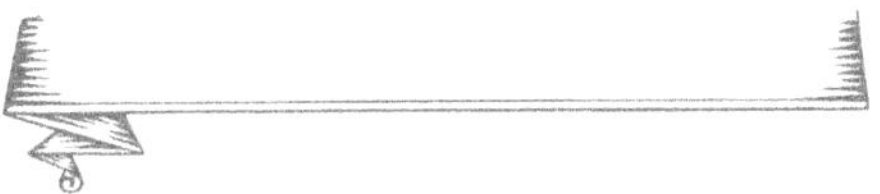

"**B**e careful," my new friend called out to me as I was walking out her front door.

"Um, okay," I called back.

It seemed strange to me, a young man raised in central Wisconsin, for my new southern friend in Tennessee to tell me to be careful.

I was only driving two miles to my newly rented house. On top of that, it was getting late in the evening, which meant there would be almost no traffic on my small town's streets.

What I didn't know then was that my friend's words had nothing to do with my driving habits. I was living in the South now, and those words encompassed a great deal more meaning.

My family is not physically affectionate. I remember my dad hugging me once in my teens, and once more in my early twenties, when I was leaving Wisconsin to start a new life in Tennessee. Things with my mom were much the same.

I always knew my parents loved me. There was always a roof over my head, good food to eat, and clean clothing to wear.

Expressing affection with words or touch was just not something that my midwestern family did.

But then, life changed me.

It was a bit of a struggle in middle school when I became close friends with a group of kids who were huggers. They liked to hug hello and goodbye almost every day.

I wasn't sure how to take all that physical contact, especially since it had never been a part of my previous life, but in time I learned to enjoy it.

Jump forward a few years, and the South is full of people who like to hug you. Men, women, children—it doesn't matter. Hugging each other is part of southern life. You hug to say hello, nice to meet you, goodbye, or I'm proud of you.

Sometimes you hug for no reason at all.

Yes, people in the South have it right. They're not afraid to tell you they love you nor afraid to show it.

You're probably wondering, what does affection have to do with saying, "Be careful"?

In time, I came to realize that saying, "Be careful," had no connection with doing something safely. It's an expression of affection, another way to tell someone you love them, especially when saying goodbye.

Recognizing what these words meant opened my eyes to some other ways that others might say, "I love you," using other words.

Some years later, I became friends with a couple from Connecticut. Every time we drove past the husband's parent's house, I noticed he would beep his horn three times.

Early one morning, thinking how much his parent's neighbors must hate the habit, I asked him why he didn't just beep once. I figured he was only doing it to let them know he was driving past.

"Beep, beep, beep," he started. "One, two, three. For my family, it's our way of saying, 'I love you,' even if we can't use words."

When he was a small child, his mother started the tradition. Any sound they made three times was their way of expressing their love for each other.

It's a tradition I adopted in my life.

If you keep your eyes and ears open, there are lots of other ways people say, "I love you," without saying the words.

Sometimes it's a text or phone call that says, "I just wanted to check on you."

Other times, it's the thoughtful touch to your arm or shoulder. It could be the dinner that your husband prepared to surprise you or the quiet smile from your wife at the end of the day.

You might see the words in your child's latest art project or in the fresh-baked cookies your friend dropped off.

If you're alert, you may find that people are telling you how much they care far more often than you thought.

Day 2 | Focus on Your Family (Chosen Family Counts)

My favorite childhood memories revolve around the trips my family took to a friend's lakeside cabin. The place was small, with a leaky roof and a funky brown goo that ran down one wall, but it was paradise to me.

The times we went to the cabin, we were happy. Our family was together. No one was running off to work or to hang with friends. We ate together, swam together, and played games together after dark.

Now that I'm an adult, I realize how rare those times were. In our busy lives, it's hard to find the time to be together as a family. As the years passed, my family drifted apart. While I'm close to my sister and care for my aging parents, I miss those cabin days.

Over the years, my family changed from the group who went to that north woods cabin to the friends I met who were on similar journeys. Those kindred spirits are now integral parts of my chosen family.

When you add the right friends to your chosen family, you feel a sense of home you may not have experienced before. Maybe your home life was tough growing up, so the word family was painful for you. With a chosen family, you can choose to add only those people who make your life better.

My family was far from perfect, but there are many wonderful memories like our cabin trips. Even so, it's often my chosen family I cling to the most.

It's critical to have people in your life who get you and let you be yourself. The most valuable members of my chosen family also fight some sort of mental illness. Knowing they understand the dark and twisty things inside me creates an unbreakable bond.

Think today about your family, whether related by blood or carefully chosen. Who lets you be your authentic self? Who is there for you every time you call? Add them to your positivity list for today.

No matter what our lives look like, family is the one constant we can all rely on. They're the people who know us best and love us unconditionally. So if you're feeling lost or alone, remember that you always have a family to come home to. Because at the end of the day, family is everything.

Journal Prompt: What does family mean to you? Who are the most important members of your family? Why?

Creative Writing Prompt: Pick five random animals and imagine they are a family. Write a story about them spending an afternoon together.

Forgive Your Parents

Preface: I was sexually abused as a child. This chapter isn't about the abuse, but it's an important piece of this story. Neither of my parents was the abuser.

I've seen many social media posts that give me hope for the future. There was a woman who was considering ending things and then received an outpouring of hundreds of strangers telling her that her life was worth living. A mom posted about how she was the worst mother ever, and dozens of other moms reached out to tell her she wasn't terrible or alone in how she felt. A man posted about how worthless he felt. Tweets came flying in, telling him he shouldn't listen to those voices in his head because they were wrong.

As many in the world become more attune to promoting good mental health, we hear more expressions like:

- It's okay to be a work-in-progress.
- Forgive yourself.
- It's not how many times you fall down, but how many times you get up.

We're learning the value of forgiving ourselves. Doing so makes it easier to forgive others, and many are taking the steps to spread forgiveness.

One troubling trend I see, though, is that with all the forgiveness and acceptance of flaws, there seems to be one group that's being left out—our parents.

The mindset seems to be that parents' mistakes are eternal. They made poor decisions, and those actions should lead to a lifetime of punishment. But I ask, why? Should you forgive your parents? If so, how can you do it? Here's how I did it.

Let's start by acknowledging that some parents don't merit forgiveness. The parents who keep their kids in cages or locked in basements or punish them with cigarette burns, those parents don't deserve forgiveness. Parents who purposely neglect their children, leaving them without food, clothing, or shelter, don't warrant forgiveness either. And the parents who sexually harm their children, well, I don't think there's a place bad enough to send them.

Fortunately, most of us didn't have those parents. Instead, we had parents just like us. One, two, three, or four imperfect people, trying their best in the circumstances they were in. Yet many people don't want to forgive their parents for the mistakes they made.

Why is it okay for a stranger to say they are still a work-in-progress at eighty years old, but for you not to accept the mistakes of your father? Why can a character in a movie pull at your heartstrings as she tries to make amends, yet your mother remains forever punished? I know I was rooting for Vivi in *Divine Secrets of the Ya-Ya Sisterhood*, yet not offering the same grace to my mother.

I'm no stranger to the subject of forgiving your parents. I left home at 20, largely because I didn't think I could forgive my parents. My parents made a lot of mistakes. Perhaps the worst was being too trusting about where they let me spend the night. Those mistakes scarred me forever.

Around the time I turned 20, memories of past abuse resurfaced. It made no sense. Something I couldn't remember yesterday was now all-consuming today.

A friend described it this way. Children don't have the capacity to deal with horrific events. To protect itself, their brain throws those experiences in a closet. As we get older and stronger, the closet door spills open and all those nightmares tumble out.

My closet burst open with such force that it rattled my entire life. As I remembered more of my nightmares, I became consumed with anger. My parents had failed me and allowed the worst to happen. My only option was to abandon them and never speak to them again.

With fight-or-flight in full-alert status, I ran away. I ran from my family, my home, and my childhood friends. I moved 900 miles, hoping to escape my memories.

In time, I found myself in therapy, an experience I recommend to everyone. During those six years, I peeled back the many layers of me. Removing the layers helped me learn to forgive the parts of me I hated. Forgiving yourself is a long process, and my journey is far from over.

Therapy taught me to look at the terrible decisions I made in my life. There are a lot of them. My therapist helped me realize some of my worst decisions resulted from things that happened to or around me. I still made the choices, but there were prior thought patterns and behaviors that made each option look like the right one.

As I worked through therapy, my therapist pointed out the times I was deceiving myself. She kept telling me, "The only way past the pain is through it."

The process was excruciating, but taught me to forgive myself. I was an imperfect being, an eternal work-in-progress. I couldn't expect perfection from something that was so imperfect.

It didn't happen quickly, but I started to apply what I was learning about myself to my parents. The proverbial light slowly came on.

My parents weren't a monstrous couple. They were two imperfect beings, fighting against their own histories and circumstances. Each of them made decisions, some of which harmed us as their children, but were based on what they felt was right. They had their own pasts that defined what seemed like the right steps forward.

As I learned to view my parents as ordinary people, my attitude toward them changed. I had been willing to offer more grace and mercy to strangers than to the two people who raised me. It was the start of real change.

For most of us, the pain caused in childhood doesn't go away. There are words your parents said and things they did that will always be with you. There's no escaping that.

I had a right to be mad at my parents. They made some terrible decisions, and those choices hurt me.

You also may be justifiably angry about how you were hurt. But, just because you have a legitimate cause for complaint, it doesn't mean you should continue to hold your parents' mistakes against them.

So the question is, how do you forgive your parents? Here are three things that helped me.

The first step in forgiving your parents is changing how you see them. A change in perspective can reveal very different people.

Take some time to look at your parents from a new angle. Rather than a palette filled with all your memories and emotions from the past, pull your parents out of your family picture. See them as if they were two human beings you didn't know. What was their past? What events shaped them? How were they treated along the way? What hardships did they overcome?

As you look at your parents from outside of the family circle, you may find the seeds of forgiveness sprouting. Your mother was beautifully broken, and she passed some of her hurt on to you. Your father's childhood damaged him and he treated you the only way he knew how.

Those imperfect beings with all their scars deserve a second look. They are worthy of mercy and redemption.

The second step in forgiving your parents is letting go of the past. This one will take some time, and you will slip backwards from time to time, but you can start again.

My parents' poor choices lead to me being sexually abused. In their defense, they didn't know. Had I told them the first time, it wouldn't have happened again.

I was a broken child and didn't know how to tell anyone. Instead, my parents didn't learn the details until I was 20, and by then, I was too angry to talk about it. They couldn't fix it.

In hindsight, they should have been wary of the places they let me go. However, what they saw then was a very different picture of what turned out to be reality.

I had to accept that what happened to me wasn't my parents' fault. Yes, they could have protected me better, but they didn't know the danger. They weren't the abuser.

I don't have children of my own. It's impossible for me to say how I would have acted in the same situation. I might have made the same decisions, especially based on what my parents knew then.

No matter how much pain I felt, my parents couldn't do anything to change what happened. It's no different from putting a valuable crystal vase on an unstable table. A careless person bumps the table and the vase crashes to the ground. The damage is unfixable. Yet, the person who placed the vase had no intention of harming it.

That was my parents. They made a poor choice and placed me somewhere I wasn't safe, but it didn't look dangerous. Like the crystal vase, a careless person broke me. I can't fault the person who put me there. Nothing can change the fact that I fell to the ground. Dwelling in the past was not helping anyone.

A third way to forgive your parents is to practice gratitude. Even parents who make lots of mistakes teach valuable lessons to their children. Most children receive food, clothing, and at least some love. You may not have had a perfect childhood, but there are reasons to be grateful. As I worked through my pain, I could see many reasons.

My parents were hard workers. My siblings and I always had a roof over our heads, clean clothes on our backs, and good food in our bellies.

They did not leave us alone for days or deprive us of an education. Our parents did their best to teach us how to be respectable people, to be productive members of society, and to have faith to see us through the tough times.

When I concentrated on the good things, it was easier to forgive my parents. The more I looked for positive things, the more good I found.

I remembered how my mother read to me for hours when I was small. Her patient attention caused a love for books and writing to flourish inside me. That I'm a writer today is because of what she did.

My dad didn't teach me all the things I wanted to learn. In fact, I'm still not confident in my ability to work on engines even though he could fix almost everything. Instead, he taught me about doing hard work. He helped me understand that my word means something, and that "any job worth doing is worth doing right." I have succeeded in every job I had because of the work ethic he taught me.

Best of all, my parents taught me about faith. If your faith is strong, you can face any trial successfully. For my parents, one of their worst trials was almost losing me. Not only did I flee from their home and move 900 miles cross-country, but a couple of years later, mental illness inspired a suicide attempt. Had I not survived, the pain of grief would have crushed them.

My parents refused to give up. Although I never made it easy for them, we eventually reconciled. They are now my closest friends, and I spend part of every day caring for their daily needs.

I'm still here, writing these words for you to read. As God saw my parents through that trying time, he's also seen us through everything since. Forgiveness brought us back together so we could love each other again.

Forgiveness is vital for a happy life. Holding on to hurt feelings and painful memories will only harm you. By learning to let go of those things, you set yourself free. You can learn to forgive by changing your perspective, leaving the past behind, and looking for reasons to be grateful.

Whether your parents are still living or have already fallen asleep in death, set them free. They were works-in-progress, but likely did the best they could in their circumstances. Choose to see them as beautifully broken and be thankful for the good things they did. Freeing them will free you as well.

Day 3 | Accept Yourself To Be Successful Living With Bipolar Disorder

Do you ever feel you're not good enough? That you have to put on a face for the world and be someone that you're not? If so, you're definitely not alone. Millions of people deal with this issue every day.

Many refer to it as impostor syndrome, but with bipolar disorder, it's often something more. Mental illness lies to you, and a negative internal chorus chants about your worst traits.

It's easy to get stuck in a spiral of negativity or to feel like you have to pretend to be someone else. I did the same thing for a long time. I hid my pain inside and did all I could to stop people from learning I had bipolar disorder. And it made me miserable.

Years were wasted with me hiding the things I loved and concealing my feelings behind a fake smile. It was only when I started accepting all of the parts of me that I started to feel comfortable in my own skin.

To be successful, you must be yourself. There is no need to hide your true nature or to put on a facade. If you're living with bipolar disorder, it's especially important to accept yourself for who you are.

Bipolar disorder is a tough foe to fight. Your moods can swing to extreme ends. You can go from feeling happy and energized to feeling completely depressed and hopeless. Sometimes the swing happens within a few days, and occasionally, within a few hours.

When you're dealing with dizzying highs or devastating lows, it's easy to feel like you're not good enough. It feels necessary to put on a mask for the world and be someone that you're not. Except that it's not true. You are good enough, just the way you are, and you don't have to pretend to be anyone else.

One of the best things you can do is accept yourself for who you are. Accept that you have bipolar disorder and that it's a part of you. Once you do that, it becomes a lot easier to deal with the ups and downs of life. It also becomes easier to find the support and help that you need.

Of course, successfully treating bipolar disorder takes a lot more than just acceptance, but it's a vital step. It's only after you own all parts of you that you can begin to change.

If you're struggling to accept yourself, I encourage you to reach out for help. Speak to those closest to you and your mental health care team. Do an internet search and find resources to help you.

Never forget, you are not alone in this fight. Millions of people are living with bipolar disorder and accepting themselves for who they are. Let their strength empower you to do the same.

Journal Prompt: What do you think it takes to be successful? Do you believe that being yourself is an important part of success? Why?

Creative Writing Prompt: Imagine you wake up tomorrow and your skin is bright green and destined to stay that color for the rest of your life. Why is it that color? How will your life change as a result? Will you hide or show your new hue to the world?

Watch The Butterfly Circus

Most of my life, I didn't share my writing with the world. Even though I've been writing for almost as long as I could hold a pen, there was a part of me that felt my writing was never good enough to share. It's a lesson I thought of after watching the short film, *The Butterfly Circus.*

The Butterfly Circus is a short film on YouTube that highlights the importance of looking at the things you can do versus the things you can't. The 22-minute film focuses on a group of circus performers.

One character, living with no arms or legs, copes with a life of abuse and negativity. He feels incapable of improving his life, so he puts up with the worst of the world around him.

This man feels he has no self-worth. When another character recognizes his value, the man starts to believe he is more and can be more. Then, with each new success, he builds confidence and learns how valuable he really is and just how much he can do.

I can't be sure if mental illness caused my lack of confidence or if it's just simply part of being a writer. For whatever reason, for a long time, I felt like I had nothing of value to share.

Then, a few years ago, I decided maybe I was wrong. So I started a blog and shared some of my thoughts.

A funny thing happened. People responded to my writing.

Originally, I blogged under a pen name. I was afraid to share my real name with people because I didn't want to be judged. While there is some freedom in writing under a pseudonym, there are also a lot of restrictions.

Creating a persona means you can never truly be yourself. It also means most of your work has to stand alone. Your readers can never get to know you, because the fictional you doesn't really exist. The wall of anonymity creates a divide between you and your readers that I never closed.

That first blog taught me how my words could affect others. In time, it led to me creating a new blog, Speaking Bipolar, and to sharing my writing on sites like Medium, Substack, and NewsBreak.

I stayed stuck for years because I focused on what I thought I couldn't do. Instead of recognizing that I could write, and had been doing it for decades, I decided I wasn't capable.

Then one day, a friend of mine shared a link to *The Butterfly Circus*.

The troubled man in the movie starts out stuck in his mind, thinking only about the things he couldn't do. It wasn't until someone took an interest in him that he realized maybe he could be more.

While it would be wonderful if all of us had a hero come along who would take an interest in us, sometimes we have to be our own hero. We may have to prove to ourselves what we can do, and then the world will see what we are.

This is especially hard when you have a mental illness. Bipolar disorder often makes me believe only the worst things about myself. I know those things aren't true, but my illness makes me believe they are.

Like the man in the movie, I'm repeatedly stuck on the things I can't do. Even though I've been successfully blogging for years now, most days, I don't believe my writing is any good. I don't think my words have any value or that anyone wants to read them. And often I'm wrong.

In *The Butterfly Circus*, the character only makes a transformation after he forces himself to see what he can do. Once he gained one success, he felt confident to try more.

That's true for all of us. When we prove to ourselves what we can do, then our success propels us forward so we can do even more.

If there's an activity you want to do but you're afraid to start, I encourage you to watch this film. Think of yourself as you watch the character's transformation. Then think about what you can do.

You don't have to jump off a diving board on your first day, but you have to start somewhere. Take a step and see what you can accomplish. The results may surprise you.

Day 4 | Focus on the Small Things

Can you move a mountain? With enough time, I believe anyone can.

Confucius said, "The man who moves a mountain begins by carrying away small stones."

Breaking things down into their smallest parts makes them easier to handle. I learned this lesson as a teenager.

Each year, my family celebrated my parent's anniversary by giving each other gifts. It was the only day we were all together and getting along. Well, at least for a few minutes.

Even though it was their anniversary, my parents would give each of us five children a gift. One year, though, instead of individual gifts, they opted for one special gift: a pool table.

We loved the pool table and spent hours playing every game you can imagine, including a sadistic one where you placed your fingers on the side of a pocket to see if you could move faster than the person rolling a high-speed ball your way.

When it came time to move away from my childhood home, I mourned the thought of leaving the pool table behind. I couldn't imagine there was any way to take that eight-foot masterpiece with us, but I was wrong.

The same company that sold us the table came and carefully took it apart. They then reassembled it in our new house. The pool table was only movable when in its smallest pieces.

Being diagnosed with a mental illness is a lot like being given a pool table. Bipolar becomes a huge fixture in your life that you need to figure out how to carry. You can only do it by carrying small pieces.

Tackle your mental health like you would move a mountain. Move the small stones: take your medication, eat nutritious food, and spend time outside. Every positive step you take is progress and a win you should celebrate.

Never downplay the tiny steps you take to care for your mental or physical health. If all you did today was take your meds and keep living, you're moving your mountain.

The next time you're outside, find a little stone. Remind yourself how the tiny object in your hand was once a part of something much bigger. You just moved part of a mountain. What else can you do today?

Journal Prompt: What progress have you made in caring for your mental health? What small stones do you think you should move next? Why?

Creative Writing Prompt: You've been given a quest to retrieve a great treasure, but it's hidden at the top of a mountain. Write a story about your journey up the mountain. What do you find when you get to the top?

Explore the Power of the Little Steps

When was the last time you looked at a piece of grass?

There's not much to it. Pluck a blade of grass and it decomposes so quickly that in a few days there's no evidence it was ever there. But that tiny plant can create great things.

One summer, a yellow-billed starling built a refuge in one of my office windows. There was a sign covering the window on the outside, and on the inside was our file room. Like a bird version of an ant farm, we got to see every step of our feathered friend creating a home. Every time I went to retrieve a file, I thought about the lesson behind the glass.

My bird friend started building in the spring. For a while in early summer, we thought she abandoned her mission as we saw little progress. Then, in about mid July, she was back at it again.

Piece by piece, she built what became her winter home.

Every time I looked at the window, I marveled at how much work she did. Likely never carrying more than two or three pieces of straw during a flight, she collected thousands of pieces. Each day, the black bird plucked blade after blade of dried grass, brought them to her future home, and then stamped them down to make a warm barrier against the coming winter.

Each blade of grass seemed like nothing until they were knitted together. The nest was a living illustration of the value of small steps.

When you're working toward a goal, it's easy to become fixated on the end goal, but the daily steps are just as important.

For example, I'm putting together my next book. I hope it leads to a series of books, but for today, it's just one.

Writing and editing a book is an overwhelming process. There are hundreds of hours of work put in behind the scenes. Some days, the enormity of the task is more than my brain can take, and I have to step away for a bit.

When I read *Charlotte's Web* as a child, I began my dream of writing a book. Over the years, it became a bucket-list item. I still wanted a book, but it was a goal I perpetually put off.

Then one day, after publishing hundreds of online articles, I realized I had already written a book. Maybe two or three. It was just a matter of putting the right posts together to form a collection.

Creating a book is a lot like building a nest. Words add up, one by one, until they become paragraphs and chapters. Chapters strung together make a finished manuscript.

Just like my feathered friend, my book isn't happening overnight. Hundreds of tiny writing and editing sessions have created the content, and many more hours will go into organizing and refining it.

Every moment I spend on the project is worth it. Most of them don't feel exciting. However, I know how amazing it will feel to hold a physical copy of my finished book in my hands. Each step in getting there is equally important.

Too often, we forget the value of the little steps. It's only when we reach our goals that we look back and reflect on all the effort that brought us there.

Take some time to appreciate each step now. Whatever you are doing—writing a book, losing weight, quitting an unhealthy habit—focus on the small steps. Create tiny goals you can reach each day. Move just a few pieces of grass.

Before you know it, you'll have your own nest.

Day 5 | Appreciate Life, Even With a Mental Illness

Life may not always feel positive.

When I wake up to a dark bipolar cycle, I know the day will torment me like an angry dog. Severe bipolar depression days turn my skies black and suck all happy emotions from my heart.

Most days, however, just waking up is a reason to be happy.

Viewing life as a positive thing might mean changing the way you see it. One key to living successfully with mental illness is to learn to say goodbye to the life you thought you would have. Life might not be what you planned, but it can be just as good.

Here are some steps to help you get there.

Focus on the Good

FIND COMFORT IN THE positive moments, even if they're small.

Choose to see joy in the everyday things: a sunny day, a hot cup of coffee, or a thrilling book. These moments matter and make up your life. Just seeing the bright red cardinal outside my bathroom window each morning is enough to start my day on the right path.

It's also crucial to do things to make you happy and help you cope with your mental illness.

Exercise

YOU DON'T NEED ME TO tell you exercise is good for you. We all know it even when we don't want to believe it. Physical activity can help improve your mood, fight off anxiety and depression, and give you more energy. Even a five-minute walk can improve your mindset.

When stress at work gets to be too much, I take a break and walk around the block. It's amazing how much good a few moments of strolling outside can do for your mental health.

Eat Healthy

WHAT YOU EAT AFFECTS how you feel. Eating unhealthy foods can make bipolar disorder symptoms worse. However, healthy choices can improve the way you feel and your overall mood.

I get how tough it is some days to eat well. I'm the first to reach for the potato chips on a stressful day, but I'm also aware of the consequences. Eating a balanced diet with lots of fruits, vegetables, and whole grains can lift your spirits and give you more energy.

Get Enough Sleep

THERE'S A REASON WHY they use sleep deprivation in torture. Even a person with perfect mental health will quickly sink into darkness and despair after a few days of no sleep. When you're starting with bipolar disorder or another mental illness, sleep is even more essential.

Sticking to a good sleep schedule is essential for good mental health. When you get enough rest, it's much easier to maintain your mood, mental clarity, and concentration. A good night's sleep can also help reduce stress and anxiety. For the best results, try to go to bed and get up at the same time every day. Yes, even on your days off.

Talk to Someone You Trust

IT'S EASIER TO CARRY a load when someone is there to help you. Talking to someone you trust about your mental health can make the hard days easier to handle. A non-judgemental listener can help you understand your thoughts and feelings. It's especially beneficial if they understand your mental illness, but even if they don't, a friend willing to listen is worth their weight in gold.

Make Time for Yourself

YOU ARE A PERSON OF value and deserve time just for you. Pick an activity that makes you happy, even if it's something small, such as a crossword puzzle. It's healthy to take a few minutes for a positive task, like taking a bubble bath or reading your favorite book.

These are just a few ideas to get you started. As you try each tip, pay attention to how it makes you feel. When you find an activity that works well for you, schedule time to do it often. Part of self-care includes doing what makes you happy.

Today, think about the good in your life–the people, the places, the food, etc. Let those pleasant thoughts move you to a place of happiness. For me, that list includes my closest friends, the beach, and a four-cheese lasagna. I love me some pasta and cheese.

My mom loves to say, "Where there's life, there's hope." Today might not be a good day, but better days will come again. Focus on the good in life and it will help keep you going.

Journal Prompt: How is your life different from how you imagined it would be? In what ways is it better?

Creative Writing Prompt: For the next 24 hours, you can be anyone else–past, present, or future. Who would you be? Write a story about how you would spend your day as that person.

Never Stop Trying To Be Better

"Had a bad day again..." So starts the iconic song, *Bad Day*, by Fuel. It's one of the songs in the soundtrack of my life.

Bad days are part of having a mental illness. Sometimes it's a bad day because you made a poor decision. Perhaps you slipped back into the habit of self-harm, lost impulse control, or gave in to substance abuse.

The weight of your mistake can be crushing. Yet, as bad as it might be, you haven't truly failed until you stop trying to be better.

Every morning, you receive the wonderful gift of a new day. It's a chance to start over and do better than yesterday.

When I was still struggling with self-harm, mornings were bleak. I would wake up to see the results of my work, and be devastated that I had slipped into old patterns again.

It took a lot of time and hard work before I was able to see how each day has its own possibilities. Just because I chose poorly yesterday doesn't mean today has to go the same way. Like the ocean cleansing the sand, I could decide each day how to make my sandcastle.

Every day gives us the opportunity to make better choices. Those decisions can be completely different from what happened yesterday.

It took years for me to stop the habit of self-harming. I'd love to say I never feel the urge anymore, but that's untrue.

Even though the desire is still there, it's been over a decade since the last time I have engaged in any type of self-harming activity. That victory brings me a lot of joy and reminds me I have the power to change. I hope it strengthens you to believe success is possible, too.

I wouldn't be here if I had given up anywhere along my journey. Even in the darkest times, I didn't let my missteps destroy me. Instead, no matter how many times I slipped, I started the next day with the belief I could do better–be better. In time, I proved that belief was true.

You can do the same. It doesn't matter what you did yesterday or even earlier today. Tomorrow is a new day. You can do better. You only fail when you stop trying.

Day 6 | Try Writing Poetry to Boost Your Mental Health

You might be tempted to skip this chapter. Perhaps you think you hate poetry, so the thought of writing it is unappealing, but I ask you please to stick around for a few minutes.

I love poetry. Not all of it, mind you, but enough to call myself a poet.

There's something magical about poetry. Thoughts and emotions have to be revealed rhythmically, sticking to the pattern chosen at the start. There's a limit to the words you can use, and that limitation holds the power.

When you write in a journal, you are free to write in any way you choose. You can use endless words or repeat the same ones over and over. There's no structure.

Poetry, though, has rules. Whether you stick to a rhyming scheme or adhere to a syllable count, not every word that pops into your head is useful.

I will never be a great poet, and I'm good with that. Most of the poetry I write and share has nothing to do with attaining fame. Instead, I write poetry to express the feelings I can't explain any other way.

The following chapters will introduce you to some of my poetry. *You Call Me* explores grief and lingering feelings I expected to pass years ago. *Beast Within* examines the internal realities of living with bipolar disorder and how it can feel like a monster inside you. *I Don't Want to People Today* reveals the thoughts that frequent my mind as an introvert. Finally, in *Darkness is Coming*, I describe how it feels when you know your depression is returning.

The beauty of each poem is that choosing to write rhythmically changed the way I expressed myself. It forced me to dive deeper, to examine the hidden feelings, and explain them in simple terms.

Sometimes, the only way to express how you feel is with poetry. I thought I was alone in this until a fellow Instagrammer posted a similar thought in her feed. Dozens of mental illness warriors commented on her thread about the power of writing poetry.

Your assignment for today is to write a poem. Explore what you're feeling at this moment. What is making you happy or sad or causing you anxiety? Then pick a poetic structure and write.

This poem is for you. No one needs to ever see your words unless you choose to share them. This poetry sandbox is for you to play in, so use it as you will.

Start a poem and see where it takes you.

Journal Prompt: What's your favorite poem? How does it make you feel? If you dislike poetry, write about why you feel that way. Where did your aversion to poetry start?

Creative Writing Prompt: Two people can only speak in rhymes. One hurt the other. Write the verbal fight they have.

You Call Me

You call me late
Where phantoms wait
The sound surrenders sleep
Midnight to blame
Your voice, my name
Echoes disturb the sheep

I smell your scent
Memories vent
Old dreams invoke your face
Though nothing real
My senses steal
The world a foreign place

No one ever
Near as clever
Revealed lunar eclipse
My name the same
Your silly game
Secrets escaped your lips

SCOTT NINNEMAN

Now twelve years gone
The vacuum strong
A void no one can fill
Nighttime sadness
Cold pain madness
Emptiness I can't kill

The ocean's tide
A longboard ride
Everything you once loved
Reminds my mind
Thoughts intertwined
Breaking from where they're shoved

With each full moon
King David's tune
I sense your gentle touch
Just out of reach
Dimensions breach
Your essence past my clutch

Time hasn't healed
This wound revealed
Repaired the bleeding ache
A decade past

Black bruises last
Nothing sedates its wake

The waves call out
Crashing, devout
Their chorus sings your song
Move on from here
Relinquish fear
Believe new love not wrong

Stuck here I stand
Forever banned
To where I once held you
Emotions trick
Impulses quick
Yet here I stay in queue

So call my name
Secure your claim
I'll gladly forsake sleep
For in that tone
My heart you own
And silently I weep

Beast Within

I hate this thing that lives in me
A raging force I cannot flee

A snarling beast with razor teeth
A grievous fiend hidden beneath

I hate the song it loves to sing
Despair and angst both loud will ring

Cruel voices chant my ev'ry flaw
Consuming thoughts its fangs will gnaw

I hate the pain that floods my mind
Faces I've hurt all intertwined

Mistakes I've made each time I failed

A past that haunts and keeps me jailed

I hate the arms that crush my chest
They shake my soul to block my rest

Forbidding breath or calls for aid
Reminding all there's debts unpaid

I hate the growls, menacing threats
The images it ne'er forgets

The pounding of it's thund'rous feet
The lies it tells ever repeat

I hate the rage that makes me scared
Banishing those who might have cared

The way it turns my heart to ice
Yet holds me fast within its vice

I hate the storm induced by it

SPEAKING BIPOLAR'S 30 DAYS OF POSITIVITY

Rampage of words, each one will hit

Cold swirling hail, destructive winds
Black rising sea never rescinds

I hate the chains that keep us bound
One life, two hearts, until the ground

Our past and fate forever joined
These words of ours forever coined

Of man and Beast, which one survives?
It seems to be the one who thrives

The sharpened teeth dull gentle eyes
Ever as fierce despite my cries

This beast is mine, it lives in me
I dream in vain, it will not flee

We share one mind until the end

SCOTT NINNEMAN

So I must learn to call it friend

I Don't Want to People Today

I don't want to people today
I don't want to come out and play

I don't want to travel outside
I don't want to confront the tide

I don't want to see your outfit
I don't want to know your secret

I don't want to fake a nice smile
I don't want to hang out awhile

I don't want to give you applause
I don't want to obey your laws

I don't want to get too upset

I don't want to need to forget

I don't want to give you a ride
I don't want to protect your pride

I don't want to stand in your line
I don't want to toast with red wine

I don't want to sample your food
I don't want to fix your bad mood

I don't want to hear while you hum
I don't want to know why you're glum

Today's too much, I cannot play
Please don't make me people today

Darkness Is Coming

Darkness is coming
Lurking on hillsides
Dancing amidst clouds
Triggering landslides

Darkness is coming
Gathering strangers
Brewing up trouble
Hiding old dangers

Darkness is coming
Stealing the sun's light
Passing out shadows
Dispensing its blight

Darkness is coming
Summoning your fate
Calling in orders
Deciding the date

Darkness is coming
Commanding all thoughts
Strangling desires
Disconnecting dots

Darkness is coming
Whispering fresh lies
Altering beliefs
Silencing allies

Darkness is coming
Freezing the scorched earth
Dulling sharp edges
Blurring priceless worth

Darkness is coming
Battling each protest
Canceling parades
Closing the hope chest

Darkness is coming
Harvesting power
Welcoming sadness
Making one cower

Darkness is coming
Insisting it's crowned
Numbing all feeling
Wetting arid ground

Darkness is coming
Cementing the night
Embracing despair
Tightening its bite

Darkness is coming

Day 7 | Give Gratitude as a Gift to Yourself and Others

Growing up, I knew a woman who had lost much of her mobility to polio. She needed crutches to walk and hobbled about, swinging her legs out wide with every step.

Her husband didn't appreciate her, and neither did her three sons. Still, she worked tirelessly to provide a warm and welcoming home. She did the shopping, the cooking, and cleaning, and still found time to do good things for others.

I never told her how much I admired her until I moved away. Then, late one night in a bipolar frenzy, I poured out my heart to her in a letter. What I never expected was that my letter became one of her most prized possessions. For the first time in years, she felt seen, and she repeated her gratitude to me every time I saw her after that.

Gratitude is a gift. It's one of my favorite things to write about because practicing gratitude improves lives.

I wrote to my friend because I was grateful for the example she set. Her perseverance in the face of all her struggles made me believe I could follow her lead and overcome anything. The lesson was priceless as I learned to battle bipolar disorder. My friend's gratitude for my letter filled her with joy.

Gratitude won't cure your mental illness, but it will change your focus. When you change your focal point, your entire life changes. If you appreciate the things you have rather than thinking of the things you don't, you realize how many blessings you possess.

I recommend keeping a gratitude jar. Try to add three things you are thankful for each day. When you're having a tough day, remind yourself of all of your reasons to live by looking at your gratitude collection.

For today, focus on the one thing that makes you the most grateful. It could be a person, event, object, or anything else. Let that reason be your positive energy source for your day.

Journal Prompt: Which event in your life made you feel the most grateful? Why?

Creative Writing Prompt: In the afternoon's mail, you receive a letter that forever changes your life. Write the letter and describe the person who sent it and the reason behind it.

Keep in Mind We All Have Something To Give

"I'm indigent," a client told me one day. His shirt was in tatters from excessive wear, and the aroma following him was far from floral, but my heart went out to him. He had nothing, but was trying to do his best.

"I can't pay today unless you can take it out of my refund," he continued. His eyes told me he was expecting me to say no.

As a tax preparer, the only legal way to do what he was asking is with a refund anticipation loan, and my firm doesn't partner with a bank. Generally, we require payment before we e-file.

"Let's see what we can do," I told him with a smile, and I took the few documents he had with him. His response made me wonder how long it had been since anyone had smiled at him.

A quick scan through his papers told me he was due a refund, and I thought to myself how I would not charge him as a kindness. It surprised me what he said next.

"I have to pay something," he told me. "It wouldn't be right otherwise."

Looking at him for a long moment, I saw more than the ragged clothes and lack of hygiene. I noticed how his face was drawn on one side, likely the result of a stroke. As we discussed his return, I noticed as he turned his head to one side to see what I was showing him. It was clear he couldn't see out of one eye. I was more inclined than ever to supply my services for free.

I'm not a rich man. My job probably pays me an unfair wage for the knowledge and skill I have, but it's the price of living in a small town in rural Tennessee. The flexibility I receive is worth more than money.

As poor as I think I am, it cut me deep inside to see my client's annual wages at less than a quarter of mine.

"I couldn't work," he told me, thinking I needed an explanation, but I didn't. It was unmistakable the difficulties he was facing.

When I finished printing his tax return, the subject turned back to my fee.

"I must pay something," he repeated. "I can leave you something of value until I come back."

I couldn't take anything from the man, not when he already had so little, and that included not taking his pride. So, I asked him what he could afford. We decided on a price, and I filed his tax return electronically. He promised to return.

He left with me feeling unsure if he would return. Maybe he knew how to play the game and quickly caught on to which of my buttons to press, but I didn't think so. I chose to believe he was a good man trying to overcome a lifetime of misfortune.

In the end, it didn't matter if he came back. As I told him, "God will make sure I have food to eat whether you pay me or not."

A few weeks later, I couldn't hide my smile as I saw him walk through our front door, cash in hand. He stuck to his word and kept his pride intact. His example reminded me there was still a lot of good in the world.

If you have a chance to be kind today, take it. I may not have made my client's day, but he made mine. He reminded me of how much I have, and that there's always a way to help others.

Day 8 | Reflect on Memories to Reveal Their Value

The rain fell in rhythmic drops all around the screen porch. The pitter-pat of water drops falling from leaf to leaf on the nearby walnut tree soothed us into a trance.

Lizzy and I sat in silence on opposite sides of the square, glass-topped patio table that filled most of the screen porch. Occasionally glancing at each other to share a knowing smile, we mostly sat lost in our own thoughts as the melody of the rain drove us to internal depths.

After many minutes, Lizzy broke the silence and said, "A good friend is someone with which you can spend hours laughing. A best friend is someone who finds comfort in sitting together in silence."

I didn't have to say anything in reply. We said more in our silence than any words I could speak.

At the moment, we were two friends sitting peacefully in the middle of a summer rain. It was a regular day, and we did nothing but enjoy each other's company. Yet, looking back, that memory is one of my favorite times with her.

The value of those minutes was unknown at the time, but now it's a cherished memory I pray I'll never forget. I lost Lizzy in 2007, so there's no way to make new memories with her.

Memories can be a wonderful reason to be positive. My best memories are full of people and places I love. Reflecting on those warm emotions is an excellent way to start your day.

If your day is off to a rough start, take five minutes to relive one of your best memories. Truly let yourself feel it, experiencing every sound, scent, and texture. Allow the wonderful recollection to return you to the joy you felt in the past. Then, let that feeling carry you throughout your day.

It's easy to overlook the value of a moment while you're living it. Often, like my afternoon sitting listening to the rain, the best times only reveal themselves after they've passed. Be alert not to miss them.

Journal Prompt: What is one of your best memories where you did not recognize the value of the moment as it happened? Why is it a favorite memory?

Creative Writing Prompt: You have one chance to relive any moment in time, whether in your life or anyone else's. Write a story about your adventure.

Learn Why a Few Simple Letters are My Greatest Gift

Once upon a time, I wrote letters. The real pen-to-paper, put-a-stamp-on-the-envelope letters. And I wrote a lot of them.

As a writer, I love the act of writing. As an introvert, I can express my thoughts and feelings much easier with the written word than I can verbally.

For years, I was well known for my letter habit. I wrote letters to comfort others, to acknowledge their achievements, and to express my disappointment. Copies of these letters still fill binders and boxes in my home.

Not always the case, but frequent enough, many people responded with a letter of their own. Their letters are cherished treasures that I have carried with me throughout the years.

There are a few letters, though faded with time, that have become the greatest gift I ever received. They are letters from the most special person, the greatest gem my heart has ever known.

I didn't realize the significance of her letters at first, but in the years since, they have taught me valuable lessons. Here are a few of those lessons.

A fellow quote-lover, Lizzy often included meaningful quotes in her letters. One letter opens with the following.

"One is not happy without the other, nor can either of them be miserable alone. As if they could change bodies, they take their

turns in pain as well as in pleasure; relieving one another in their most adverse conditions."—William Penn

In the gentlest of ways, she revealed the course I needed to take. Back then, there was a toxic "friend" in my life.

Lizzy knew better than to tell me what to do. She was well acquainted with my stubborn nature. Instead, she chose to remain silent for a while and then wrote a letter about the value of true friends.

The letter never steered negative. In her humble manner, she explained which friends meant the most to her and why. It took years for me to understand the lesson, but it's one I will never forget.

It's easy to fall into the trap of being what we think others want us to be. Though I didn't think I was changing, Lizzy saw how I was learning to be the real me. She wrote:

> *"I admire you because you're real. That's all there is to it. You jack up as much as the rest of us. You give yourself the occasional well-deserved pat on the back. You stick your foot in your mouth just to see how it tastes. You'll give your advice even if you have to draw it out of a hat, but if you do, you always let the person know."*

She saw the real me, the person I thought I had hidden from the world. Her words taught me to let my inner self out because he is worth knowing.

It's okay to be who you really are.

One thing I admired the most about Lizzy was her ability to see the best in everyone. She always made me feel like more than I was.

Did she think I was perfect? I'll let her answer.

> *"You can tick me off with the best of them. But you know what? Somehow that's never what I remember. It's always the qualities you manifest best. That's what sticks with me."*

Memories are wonderful because we get to choose what sticks with us. She taught me to choose the positive.

One of my biggest regrets is that I did not tell her every day how much she meant to me. I think she knew—we used to joke that we shared a brain—but I still should have said it more often.

She told me so, if I had been listening.

"Thank you for being there—always there—and being you. You said today that I couldn't always read your mind... You're right. Not always. But you know what? Sometimes I don't need to. And if I don't need to, I don't even try. I realize I don't have to explain it to you. That's the way it is with us kindred spirits."

Lizzy harbored no blindness to my faults. She saw the worst and the best, but she accepted both.

There is no perfect person. We need to appreciate those we love and accept them for who they are, not who we'd like them to be. She said:

"I think this is one of the hardest parts of being an individual and handling our relationships. Figuring out, when it comes to what others teach us, what we should take note of and accept and what should be looked upon and forgotten."

Lizzy was a collector, as am I. Some of her greatest treasures were the letters she received. They taught her the value of writing.

"Who would think ink and paper could mean so much? There's something about paper that, without knowing it, draws out a person's inner soul. Almost as if it were saying, 'I dare you to write on me! Come on, show me what ya got!'"

My writing died when Lizzy did, at least, for a while. For years, my journal held the only words I wrote, and those words were far too few.

In time, I remembered the value of words. Their power sang to me. With their spirit and Lizzy's behind me, pen met paper once again, and I've not stopped since.

These few handwritten letters will remain my greatest gift, hopefully for many years to come. Their value increases each year because their author is no longer in this world. These are the last of her words I'll hear.

The thing that awes me is that there was no distance between us when she wrote these letters. There wasn't a need to put words on paper because we were always talking, always with each other.

Lizzy saw the gift of putting pen to paper, and I could never be more grateful for the time she took to sit and write.

We receive many gifts in our lifetimes. Some we cherish and pass on to our descendants, and others disappear in time. We may forget the gift itself, but the emotions long remain.

Do you have a special gift that brings you joy? Cherish it and its giver. The ones who are the most special are with us for the least amount of time.

Day 9 | Find Success by Determining To Try Once More

I close every online post and newsletter with the words, "Until next time, keep fighting."

"Keep fighting" is my mantra for a reason. It's a reminder that the next battle I fight might just be the one I win. You never know when you will achieve success.

In my journey to diagnose my Familial Mediterranean Fever, a genetic disorder that causes periodic fevers and body pain, I endured eight years of medical tests. Most test results were normal or inconclusive. Many days, I contemplated giving up, both on my health and life in general.

I imagined my symptoms were mirages conjured up by my mind, but the inflammation markers in my blood stayed 10-30 times higher than normal. Those higher numbers were something I couldn't make up.

Eventually, I met an internist willing to look deeper, and he not only figured out my illness, but started me on a treatment plan that led back to a somewhat normal life.

How did my doctor succeed where so many other professionals had failed? He was determined not to quit. He took my medical chart home with him one weekend and researched my symptoms one by one.

The effort of that amazing man changed my life. It gave me a name to describe the hell I was living in and reassured me that my mental illness had not completely robbed me of my sanity.

Before I met him, I decided the internist was going to be the last physician I saw about my mysterious symptoms. After four years and $18,000 in out-of-pocket medical expenses, there was no money left to throw at trying to find a diagnosis. Still, I decided to try one last time.

My internist admitted he was stumped during my first appointment, but he had a warm determination that made me believe this time would be different. He tried one more time and found success.

You never know what one more try will do for you. There's no counter that says, "Try 396 will be a success." You just have to keep trying.

Many believe that in his path to creating the lightbulb, Thomas Edison may have failed up to 10,000 times. Imagine if he had stopped on try 9,999. Would we have lightbulbs today?

I know you feel you've been trying for a long time. You're tired, and life is a heavy burden some days, but your success might be as close as tomorrow. You have to keep trying. Tomorrow just might be the day you create your lightbulb.

Journal Prompt: What does success look like for you? How will you feel when you achieve it?

Creative Writing Prompt: Imagine a world where light bulbs were never invented. Write a story about a day of life in that world.

Understand How the Pain in My Heart Pushed Me to Start the Speaking Bipolar Site

"And he's bipolar. You know what that means."

My boss was 10 minutes into his gossip fest. Today's victim was one of his oldest friends. I heard a litany of all the poor choices his friend had made over the years. My boss boasted of their 20-year friendship, but I couldn't help but wonder if it really was a friendship.

My boss was a good man, and not someone who generally downgraded people, but he was prone to stereotypes. His prejudice was especially evident when talking about mental illness.

Up until that day, he was unaware of my mental health struggles. Even though I was diagnosed with bipolar in 1995, it was 11 years before I told an employer, and another 12 years after that before I came out publicly with my mental health history.

"You know I'm bipolar," I said to my boss, bringing the conversation to a screeching halt.

His eyes widened as his face lost all its color.

"I didn't mean," he started.

"It's okay," I laughed. I wanted to let him off the hook, though I know now that should have been a teaching moment.

"I've made some terrible choices myself," I continued. "I just wanted you to know before you said something you'd regret."

He tried to apologize, but I just put up my hand. I wasn't comfortable then discussing my mental health, so I just wanted our conversation to end.

Fast forward to 2018, and nearly a dozen friends' suicides later, and I finally found the courage to speak up. I was ready to come out of the bipolar closet and tell my truth.

There were two suicides that were especially painful. One was my sister's ex-husband. While he and I were never close, I did care about and respect him. He was a good man and a caring father. To learn that he had chosen to take his own life was devastating.

Then, one of my friends committed suicide. It was someone my age, someone I knew had been fighting mental illness for years without treatment. I tried to broach the subject with him from time to time, but he was never willing to have the conversation. I never pushed for more. I didn't think I needed to interfere.

The morning I got the call that his brother had found him dead, a part of me wasn't surprised. I wanted to be, but I knew the look of desperation in his eyes.

Even though we'd not seen each other for a few months, I knew what was going on in his head those last few days. I've been to that point, too many times. I know that feeling when you think the only option to stop the noise inside your head is to end it all. Watchful friends saved me, but too many people aren't as lucky. No one caught on with my friend in time to save him.

Writing for me is therapy, and my friend's death made the words flow.

I'd always dreamed of being a writer, but all my hopes and fantasies revolved around fiction. I hated writing essays, and the thought of writing nonfiction held no appeal. Yet, once I started writing about mental illness, I couldn't stop.

I started to tell my story, and the *Speaking Bipolar* site was born. Now, years later, I have hundreds of online posts on my blog, Medium,

NewsBreak, and more. Most stories center around my experiences with bipolar disorder.

As a society, we don't talk about mental illness enough. We let stigmas run wild, and we reinforce stereotypes by using things like bipolar and schizophrenia as the punchline of jokes.

Neither disorder is funny.

While I choose to use a lot of humor in my writing, mental illness itself is no joke. As many as one in five people with bipolar disorder will take their own life. That's 20 percent.

If we had applied the same ratio to COVID-19, the death toll would have been over a billion. The statistics are devastating, but too often, we're still not talking about it.

I don't know about you, but I don't find that very funny.

It's especially hard for men to discuss their mental health. There's a toxic belief among many people that mental illness is a form of mental weakness. Others believe it's a lack of faith. Neither idea is correct.

Most mental disorders are caused by chemical imbalances. Mental illness is just that: an illness. It's no different from being diabetic or having heart disease. Something is wrong in the body, and you usually need medicine to fix it.

The harsher stigma on men keeps many from seeking help. When things get too dark, men like my friend and brother-in-law, opt out of life rather than tell anyone how much they're suffering.

There's no way to go back and save either man, nor the dozen of other people I've lost to this insidious enemy. I can, however, share my story.

Trembling inside, I hit publish on my first blog post in February 2018. Sleep was elusive for days as I worried about the response my writing would generate, but the world didn't end. Each line of text I wrote encouraged me to write more.

I started to tell people in my daily life about my bipolar disorder and chronic anxiety. I shared my most painful experiences, and gave my readers an inside look at what it's like to live with daily suicidal ideation. Owning that truth in public felt like climbing Everest, but I will never regret it.

Learning to be authentic taught me that I'm not alone. Many people with mental illness fight the same battles every day. Every time we see another suicide in the news, it reinforces a part of our mind that believes death is the best option, but it shouldn't be that way. Suicide is never the right answer. It's a terrifying trend we need to stop.

As I said, I'm one of the lucky ones. The worst night of my life, my chosen family rescued me. They saw the warning signs before it was too late and drove me to the hospital. Their actions will forever be a daily source of gratitude.

I can't save everyone, but by sharing my story, I might be able to save some. If even one person chooses to keep living because I shared my inner struggles, then any discomfort I feel along the way will be worth it.

I am Scott Ninneman, and I have bipolar disorder. A successful life with mental illness is possible. If I can do it, so can you. Believe in yourself.

Day 10 | Gain Power by Keeping on Through the Tough Times

Janet was an elegant woman, kind to everyone she met. She dreamed of being a mother, but life was intent on stopping her.

Just weeks after she and her husband completed work on their new house, Janet was diagnosed with cancer. Cancer is always a devastating diagnosis, but Janet's doctors told her she had just six months to live.

"You're wrong," she told them. "And I'll prove it."

The first doctor was unwilling to even try. He wrote Janet off and likely never thought of her again.

Janet found another doctor to verify the diagnosis. The second professional confirmed her outlook was grim, but he was willing to treat her. They moved forward with the hope she would beat the odds.

There were many times she wanted to give up. When the chemo stripped her of half her hair, Janet shaved the rest off. She splurged and bought herself a nice wig, but still cried every time she put it on.

"I'm going to beat this," she told us with a smile every time we saw her. And beat it, she did.

I was in my mid-teens when Janet was diagnosed. Her quiet determination and refusal to give up moved all of us. Attitude means much more than we might think.

Do you ever feel you've reached the end of your rope? Everyone does from time to time. I spend so much time at the end of mine that I'm anxious when I'm not there.

Some days life feels like too much. The kids never stop making noise. The boss criticizes everything you do. Your partner is unreasonably grumpy. You name it. Dozens of things beat you down every day, and having a mental illness on top of it only makes things worse.

When you're fighting a turbulent day, you may feel giving up is the only option. On those days, keep in mind the ocean tides. That's what Janet thought about on her toughest days.

During high tide, the sea washes in, making portions of the beach disappear. If there's a hurricane behind the high tide, the water can reach a height of 20 feet or more above its normal level, causing catastrophic destruction. The struggles in your life can feel like those destructive waves.

No matter how high the water gets, the tide eventually goes out. The clouds part, and the sun shines again. The ocean cycles and the beach returns.

If your tide is high right now, hold on. Tomorrow will be better. Tie a knot in your rope and hold on tight.

As for Janet, she beat her cancer. A year after recovery, she had a baby, and that beautiful girl grew up to be an amazing woman.

We lost Janet a few years ago. Despite what the first doctor said, her six months turned into over three decades. If you're determined to hold on, you never know what you can do.

Journal Prompt: When was your last high-tide storm? How long did it last? How did you feel when it was over?

Creative Writing Prompt: You're marooned on a secluded island with a celebrity. Who is it? Write a story about your life on the island.

Enjoy the View During Unexpected Detours

Have you ever taken a detour?

Some detours are unavoidable. Road construction or a fender-bender can suddenly close roads or exits forcing you to find a new route to your destination. However, road closures are not the only detours in life.

It may be for you that your biggest detour was when you were diagnosed with a chronic or mental illness. My bipolar diagnosis changed everything.

Maybe your detour came when a relationship ended or a job came to a conclusion. You may have even felt like your route was not only detoured but closed entirely.

As my mother likes to say, "Where there is life, there's hope."

So, how do you learn to go on after an unexpected detour? Let's look at three valuable aspects to these unexpected journeys.

Creating art or writing blog content is a great way to express yourself. At times, though, the creative juices just don't seem to flow. Writers refer to it as, "writer's block," and no doubt the mental hurdle is just as tough if you're painting pictures or molding clay or anything else.

Some years ago, I was battling writer's block. In my search for solutions to get my creativity flowing again, I stumbled upon an article that offered a unique approach.

Most of us tend to be creatures of habit. We travel the same routes, eat the same things, and wear the same clothes. We love to stick to routines.

With our tendency toward repetition in mind, the article encouraged readers to change things up. Take a different avenue to work. Try a type of food you've never had before. Buy a clothing article that is outside of your everyday style choices.

Or, in other words, take a detour.

The article went on to discuss how changing our habits can also change our thinking patterns. New thoughts–new stimulation–can lead to increased creativity.

Detours do three great things for us.

1. Force us to pay closer attention
2. Allow us to see new things
3. Offer different choices

Let's take the first one. It's all too easy to zone out while driving to or from work. You probably know the route well as you drive or walk it every day. There's not a lot of thinking involved other than normal travel considerations.

Then you see that big orange sign. It may point you to a part of town you seldom visit or onto a road you've never traveled before.

Suddenly, you are forced to pay attention to where you are going, how you are driving, and what is happening around you.

The second value you can get from a detour is the chance to see and discover new things.

Personally, literal detours have helped me discover parks, restaurants, and the coolest of little stores because I was traveling on a road I never took before.

Detours in life can do the same thing. Perhaps you never imagined living a life with chronic illness. You were sure your relationship or job would never end. But then it happened. What's next?

In January of 2018, I left an 18-year career in the insurance industry. Up until a short time before I quit, I imagined I would keep the job until I retired.

Things got ugly quickly. A revelation about my boss revealed him to be a man I refused to have my name tied to, so I turned in my notice.

I live in a small community, so insurance jobs are few and far between. My unexpected path forced me to make new choices, the third value of a detour.

Writing had long been my passion, though I never really pursued it until after I resigned from my job. I had some savings and decided it was the perfect time to try new things.

Driving detours often take us on roads that are narrower or in poorer repair than the ones we are used to traveling on. The roads may be bumpy, filled with potholes, or not even paved.

My work experience was definitely one of those bumpy roads. After eight months, it became painfully clear my writing career was not going to take off at the speed I hoped. I had to make a choice to either find a career in a different field or travel an hour each way to the closest city.

Then a door opened to a job in bookkeeping and tax preparation. It was a low-stress position (most of the year) and gave me lots of time to write.

Does the change mean my detour led to failure? It all depends on how you look at it.

During my time pursuing writing, I was able to find work for a company that connects freelance writers with blogs wanting content. While the pay was low, those writing assignments helped me sharpen my writing skills and learn how to write online content.

In addition, my new route opened up the chance for me to meet people I would not have otherwise met. Included in that number is an ever-growing list of writers who are tremendously encouraging and have a wealth of useful wisdom.

You could say that meeting new people is the fourth gift my detour has given me. It's all in how I choose to look at it.

What's your experience? Take a few minutes to think about the detours you have taken in your life. Maybe you are in the process of navigating one right now.

As you reflect back, think about the following questions:

- How has my detour helped me to have better focus in my life?

- What new things have I seen?

- Which fresh choices have opened up to me?

- Who have I met that I wouldn't know if it weren't for the change in direction?

Really ponder on those gifts over the next few days.

You may even choose to take a new detour. Try a fresh experience, eat something different, or reach out to meet new people.

Yes, it's true, detours are often unwelcome or unexpected, but that doesn't mean they have to be bad. Learn to appreciate the experiences and opportunities that each change brings into your life.

Day 11 | Find Strength in Your Weaknesses

During my life, a few things have cracked me to my core. Three of the most painful ones were when I lost all control and was finally diagnosed with bipolar disorder while in a psychiatric hospital, when my business failed and I had to learn how to start over with nothing, and when I lost my best friend to a traffic accident.

Each blow felt unsurvivable. I felt like I would disintegrate into a thousand tiny pieces. It seemed each tragic event would define me from that day forward. As is often the case, I was wrong every time.

When trials come along our road to success, it may feel like the struggle cracks our inner being. But a crack doesn't always lead to a total collapse.

Japanese culture has a wonderful art form called kintsugi that teaches us how valuable cracks can be. When a porcelain vase or cup is cracked, rather than discarding the damaged item, artists fill the crack with gold.

The crack becomes a thing of beauty. The artist makes the item unique because of the damage that was done to it. Weakness becomes the focal point of strength and elegance. The value of the broken article increases.

You are no different. Your cracks make you beautiful. Through pain and trauma, you earned each scar, but by continuing to fight, you've filled those wounds with gold.

Things along the way will knock you down, but they don't have to destroy you. Fill your cracks with gold, get up, and start fighting again. Your strength will shine and resonate with everyone around you. Just like kintsugi, your beauty will inspire others.

Journal Prompt: Write about a time when life cracked you. How did you overcome it? What strength did that experience give you?

Creative Writing Prompt: You're on a first date in an art museum. Feeling anxious, you trip over your own feet, knocking a priceless vase to the ground. What happens next?

Conquer Fear by Learning to be Strong on the Darkest Days

Fear. It's something we all live with, whether we have bipolar disorder or not. I have an anxiety disorder, so fear is a subject I think about often.

Fear can be especially powerful on dark days. When life is already overwhelming, fear jumps up and shouts, "Let me pile on a little!"

Yet, fear doesn't have to hold you back. You can fight it and learn to move forward in spite of it. But what is fear really?

One dictionary defines fear as "an unpleasant, often strong emotion caused by anticipation or awareness of danger." To me, "anticipation" is the word to really think about, at least from a mental illness perspective. Let's dive a little deeper into the subject and find ways to fight back.

7 Ways to Fight Fear

Accept Fear as Part of Life

ONE LIE BIPOLAR DISORDER tells you is that healthy people do not feel fear, at least not in the same way. While it is true mental illness can increase your fear, it's critical to remember that everyone–yes, *everyone*–feels fear.

It helps to remember that most of the things you fear never happen. Anxiety, especially with bipolar, loves to play the worst-case-scenario game, but rarely do those scenarios happen.

Hundreds of thousands of people fly in airplanes every day. Many of those people have deep-seated fears about their plane crashing. Yet, thankfully, plane crashes are rare. Other fears are often the same. Don't waste time and energy fearing something that may never happen.

Take Action

TAKING ACTION IS ONE of the best ways to overcome fear. After my best friend died in a car accident, I was afraid to drive for a long time. She died after turning left onto a highway. Subconsciously, I connected the two in my mind, and for months, found it nearly impossible to turn left from any road or driveway. The irrational fear cost me a lot in gas as I frequently drove miles out of the way just so I wouldn't have to turn left and cross traffic.

Talk therapy was a big help to me. Sharing your fears out loud or writing them in a journal will often help you to look at the fear objectively. When you look at a fear face-to-face, you can frequently move past it.

Face Fear Head-on

FACING YOUR FEARS IS a common way to overcome phobias. Often, you can't understand your fear until you look it in the eye.

A friend of mine feared snakes. This was more than a simple anxiety about running across a snake outside. Instead, she switched into panic mode just by seeing a picture or a video of a snake.

To overcome her issue, she learned to work with snakes. By looking at pictures of snakes when she knew she was safe, the images lost their power over her. She'll never be a snake handler and still doesn't like snakes, but the fear is no longer as pervasive.

Think of something you fear. Is it something you can safely face? If so, try to find a way to conquer your fear.

Think back to fears you've had in the past that no longer bother you. How did you overcome those fears? Did you have to learn something new to overcome the fear, or did you already have the strength inside to help you overcome it?

Remember Past Successes

ANOTHER STEP IN THE process of learning to overcome fear is that of learning to appreciate your successes. Adversities can mold and strengthen you if you let them. It may be that what you really need is to change your perspective to get past the thing causing your anxiety.

Every time you overcome a fear successfully, you gain confidence. The strength helps you better handle your next challenge.

Public speaking is an excellent example of this concept. Personally, I hate public speaking. However, I know the more often I stand in front of people, the easier it gets. It's a very similar experience for other fears and anxieties.

Sometimes your fear revolves around something terrible happening, like the death of a loved one. As awful and debilitating as death can be, there is still an important lesson to be learned. Each thing we survive teaches us how we can handle things bigger than we thought possible.

Losing my friend just moments after I had hung up a call with her made me feel broken and unfixable, like the Humpty Dumpty nursery rhyme. Just a few days into the grieving process, I told another friend, "If I can survive this, I can survive anything."

In the years since, nothing has been as difficult as losing her. I survived my worst nightmare, and now I know I can survive almost anything else. So can you.

Learn to Sail Your Ship

WHEN THE THINGS WE fear happen, we can learn valuable life lessons. For example, vehicle safety is improved through studying car accidents. A manufacturer may simulate thousands of crash tests when developing a new safety technology. Each one of those tests provides beneficial insight.

Think of sailing the open sea. A sailor doesn't become truly adept at sailing if he only sails on calm waters. Instead, it's the storms and winds that teach him how to navigate the waters safely.

Life is rarely full of calm waters. Accept the storms in your life and use each occasion to learn how to better sail your ship.

Look Forward

ONE HURDLE OFTEN STANDING in the way of overcoming fear is getting stuck in the past. Just because something happened before doesn't mean it will happen again in the future. When I had my worst breakdown and had to be confined to a psychiatric hospital, the fear of having to go back drove me for a long time.

In time, I learned how to manage my bipolar disorder. By sticking to a treatment plan and having a supportive care team, I've never crashed as hard again. While a tiny part of me fears it could happen again, it's not happened in nearly 30 years. I'm stronger when I look forward instead of back.

Learn from your past but only think of it as a way to help you move forward. Even if life knocks you down, you can get up again. The way tomorrow goes is always up to you to choose. You can decide to leave the past behind. Yes, bad things happen, but you don't have to stay trapped in those moments. Look forward. Move forward.

Learning to overcome fear takes time and effort, but you can do it and succeed.

Day 12 | Take Action to Find Your Happiness

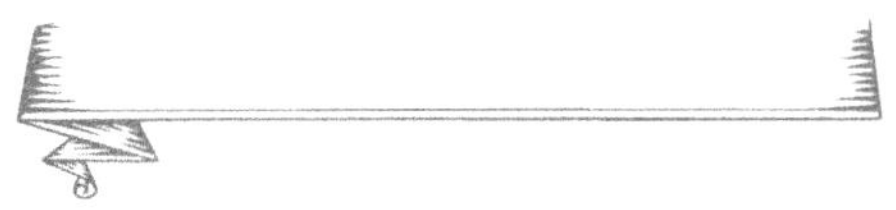

Living with mental illness means there are lots of days where it knocks you off your feet. If you choose to stay down, you will never improve. There is no guarantee that getting up will make you happier, but staying down guarantees you won't.

When you put forth the effort to improve things, whether your physical or mental health, you open the door to new opportunities. Each fresh opportunity has the potential for greatness.

Take my friend Emily. For years, she agonized over the fact she couldn't find a good husband. The more upset she got, the more isolated she became. Rarely did she go out with friends, and all the time home alone led to comfort-food binge eating and serious weight gain.

One day, Emily looked in the mirror and hated her reflection. The realities of what she was doing to herself finally clicked, and she took action.

Emily's chief concern was to improve for herself. She wasn't thinking about a potential husband or looking for admiration from her coworkers. She changed for herself because she didn't like what she had become.

She started with walking and soon turned to running. Within six months, Emily took part in her first marathon. She didn't win. In fact, she walked most of the route. She knew there was no chance she could win, but she wanted to prove to herself she could cross the finish line.

When she did, she celebrated her immense victory with some of the other participants.

Along the route, Emily met other runners who were also competing in their first marathon. Those brief introductions became strong friendships with people who had similar goals.

Emily competes in several marathons a year now. She has never finished first, but she's now able to run most of the race with a body she's happy to see in the mirror.

"It's not about the race," she told me recently. "It's about the friends who run alongside me."

Emily has those friends because she took action. Her action led her to happiness.

Spend some time today thinking about an action you can take. You don't have to run marathons, but maybe you could choose a small habit to change. For example, decide to watch less TV, eat fewer doughnuts, or spend five more minutes walking each day. The point is to make some effort to improve yourself from where you are right now.

The more you take action, the more opportunities will open up to you. It's impossible to know how your life will improve until you try to change.

Journal Prompt: What is one small habit you could change today? If you could achieve anything in the next five years, what would it be? Why?

Creative Writing Prompt: A couple meets for the first time during a marathon. Write a story about how they meet and what happens next.

Decide Who You Want To Be

Who do you want to be?

Think about it for a minute. Who do you really want to be? Are you the person you hoped to be at this point in your life?

Children are naturally dreamers. Many dream of being cowboys, spacemen, ballerinas, and so much more.

What did you dream of being as a child? What do you dream of now? Really think about it.

Today is the day to start moving in your dream's direction.

We are all surrounded by limiting beliefs, especially when we are dealing with a mental illness. But do you sometimes let those limitations restrict you too much?

It's far too easy to stop pursuing our dreams and goals because we don't have the health to get us there. Even if you are restricted, there is never a reason to give up.

After 18 years, I left a career in insurance because my employer turned out to be a disloyal individual. I couldn't imagine what was next, but I knew I had to make the change. My last job was causing so much stress it was making me anxious all the time with never-ending migraines.

My future was a blank slate, and it was up to me to choose what it would be.

My goal was to reinvent myself. I wanted to pursue a writing career and create a blog.

I am a survivor of both mental illness (bipolar disorder) and a physical chronic illness (Familial Mediterranean Fever.) Though I couldn't claim success in all areas of my life, I knew my voice could help someone else. Hence, *Speaking Bipolar* was created.

Unfortunately, neither the blog nor freelance writing led to a sustainable income. After a year, I was forced to take another "day job" as a bookkeeper and tax preparer. It was a painful blow, but I refused to give up.

Sometimes, the best way to decide how to move forward is to make a detailed evaluation of where you are right now. I did that with my blog and other online content. Then I worked with the same process for the rest of my life.

The future was hazy, but the more I broke things apart and looked inside, the more I could see what was most important to me. I knew writing had to stay an integral part of my life. The rest I would figure out along the way.

It's now years later. I'm still working as a tax preparer and bookkeeper, but writing is part of my everyday life. Hundreds of readers show up every week to read my newsletters, and there couldn't be a better feeling.

Have you ever felt like you needed to change everything? Perhaps you were facing some perplexing decision about your health or career. Is the solution really as easy as just deciding what you want?

Yes and no.

Let's face it, there are some things you will likely never be. If you are 80 years old, it's very unlikely you could start a career in space travel. Not impossible, but extremely unlikely. It would, however, be a fascinating story, so if that is you, please reach out. I would love to hear your story.

I digress.

Poor health can also restrict some of your possibilities. Living with bipolar, anxiety, and Familial Mediterranean Fever, I understand health limitations.

What is never restricted, though, is the *type* of person you are. Whether you are 12 or 836, you can always choose what type of person you will be. (Again, if you are 836 years old, I really want to tell your story. Please look me up.)

Will you choose to be forgiving? Humble? Moral? Honest? Loyal? Responsible? Kind?

The list of possibilities is endless, but the choice is yours. You are never stuck being who you are today. You can be whatever you choose.

Say it with me, "I am not stuck being who I am today."

Have you made mistakes? Are there poor choices in your past? It can't be undone, but today and tomorrow are in your power to change.

Over the next few days, take some time to think about what type of person you are. Are you the person you want to be? Are you going in the direction you desire? If not, what can you do to start moving towards being that person? What can you do today to start making the change?

It would be overwhelming to try to change everything at once. Instead, pick just one thing, one trait or goal, and make forward movement toward that goal.

Your future is in your hands. Choose wisely. You got this. I believe in you.

Day 13 | Use Courage to Tame Your Mental Illness

Growing up, my family lived in rural Wisconsin. As kids, we spent our days building snow forts, climbing trees, and running through open cornfields. It was the perfect place for children full of imagination.

With only one neighbor's house in view, nights were dark. There were no outside lights other than one near our back door.

When I was about seven, it was my job to get the mail. One cold winter night, I forgot. There were toys to play with and cartoons to watch. The mail meant nothing to me, so my job escaped my mind. When my parents asked for the mail, they weren't interested in excuses. So, I donned my puffy orange coat, knitted hat, and mittens and stepped into the night.

I wouldn't say I was afraid of the dark, but I wasn't a fan. My mind was too creative, and all I could think of were the monsters concealed in the darkness. Armed with a dim flickering flashlight, I marched into the night. There was no light on the front side of the house other than the tiny beam coming from my hand.

It felt like 100 miles to the end of our driveway, but I made it. I quickly snatched the envelopes out of the large metal box and took my first steps back toward the house.

Then I heard it, the unmistakable noise of a beast moving in the snow. My racing heart immediately knew the sound wasn't coming from tree branches rubbing together. There was no wind, so only something–something with fangs and claws–could have made the noise. The monster was moving near the blue spruce trees lining the side of our driveway.

Fear froze me in place, but I knew I couldn't stay there. I waved my light back and forth over the trees, praying I was wrong.

"Please don't let there be a monster. *Please* don't let there be a monster," I pleaded with the snow-covered trees.

Then I saw it. Two green eyes reflected back at me near the lower branches of the closest tree. I knew the eyes were connected to powerful jaws full of razor-sharp teeth.

Like a cartoon character leaving behind a trail of dust, I sped for the house. With each step, snow crunched beneath my feet and my raspy breath escaped my chest in ragged gasps. Then, I heard another sound. The beast was pursuing me and growing closer with every step.

Finally, I reached the corner of the house, the place where the light from our back porch broke the darkness. I paused for a second, but it was too long. The beast was on me... and he wanted to play.

The monster turned out to be my neighbor's black lab. Perfectly hidden in the darkness, only his eyes and a small patch of white on his throat caught the light. As he jumped around me, I laughed in hysterics; the relief inducing a sense of euphoria. My mind had made things so much worse than they were. I was in a terrifying situation, but I found the strength to do what was needed.

When was the last time you needed courage? Maybe it was when you went to the doctor and told him about all the chaos in your head. It could be the time you opened up to your partner about your social anxiety. Perhaps it was just taking this morning's meds or going to work.

Living with mental illness takes a lot of courage. There are days when even the simplest things feel impossible. Simple activities like driving, social interaction, or going to work can make you tremble inside.

Yet, as a mental illness warrior, you fight on. You know no one else is going to pay your bills or provide what your family needs. So you push yourself to do the next thing, summoning the courage you need, no matter how hard it may be. You face the monsters in the dark.

You also need courage to continue living. Bipolar disorder will tell you to give up. Fighting the dark voices takes strength. Choosing to live another day requires bravery.

For today, think about the ways you are courageous every day. You may surprise yourself at all the bravery you display on a typical day.

Life can be overwhelming, and it can feel like there are monsters everywhere, but you must go on. If today was too hard and all you did was stay alive while hiding under your blankets, that's okay. You're still here, and that's what matters. Tomorrow is a new day, and you will try again when the sun comes up.

Journal Prompt: Write about a time when you needed exceptional courage? What did the experience teach you?

Creative Writing Prompt: Write a story about someone lost in a forest at night. They receive help from an unexpected source. Who or what helps them? What happens next?

Keep a Success List to Change Your Life

Is the glass half-full or half-empty? It's the age-old question many struggle to answer.

Most of the time, for me, it depends on what's in the glass. If it's that nasty stuff you have to drink before a colonoscopy, then the glass is half full because it contains something I don't want to drink. If it's a glass of my favorite wine, then the glass is half empty, and I'm mourning the loss of it.

It's the same glass and a similar amount of liquid, yet how I look at it is completely different.

The same is true for every aspect of your life. Every event, every interaction is colored by the way you choose to see it.

When you have a mental illness, it's difficult to have a positive mindset. On the bad days, the glass is half empty no matter how hard you try to fight it. However, there is something I found that helps. My helper is the simple act of keeping a success list.

What is a success or win list? It can be a piece of paper, notebook, or digital file where you make notes of the victories in your life.

These successes don't have to be life-altering achievements, such as publishing a best-selling book or coming in first in a marathon. No, for this list, you should count every win.

- Did you take your medicine today? Win! Write it down.

- Did you take a shower and get dressed today? Win! Write it down.

● Did you eat a nutritious meal without eating too much or too little? Win! Write it down.

It's far too easy in our hectic lives to overlook our small successes. Keeping track of those wins will help you to achieve bigger goals.

How can you use a success list?

Keeping a list of your wins is different than keeping a journal. The intention isn't to mark down what happened or when. Instead, your goal is simply to have an easily accessible list to remind you of things you got right.

Depression is brutal, and when those gray skies roll in, it's hard to see anything in a positive light. When you feel like you failed at everything and there's no sense in going on, that's when it's time to look at your success list.

Those simple words will remind you that you're not a failure at everything. You succeed at many things. Keep your list handy so you can remind yourself every time you need the emotional boost.

An amazing thing starts to happen after you keep a success list for a while. Without consciously thinking about it, you start to make a positive mind shift.

Suddenly, you find the strength to face the hard things in life without being distraught about your past mistakes. Seeing where you've succeeded gives you hope that you can triumph again. Each win is like watering a tree that only grows stronger and taller with time.

That tree is you.

Spend some time creating your success list. Whether you get a notebook specifically for this purpose or simply grab a paper napkin off the table, start writing down your wins.

Don't think you have any wins to write on your list? Think harder. Anything you do can be a win. Refer to the list above.

For the next few days, as you go about your daily activities, take a moment to write down every win. Try to get at least three every day, but don't limit yourself to only three.

If, at the conclusion of the day, you don't have at least three, then reflect on your day and the things you did. If nothing else, the simple fact you're still alive is a win, so write it down.

Now you only need two more.

As time goes by, every time you need encouragement or are feeling like you're failing at everything, pull out your list and read your wins. Read them out loud if you can. There's something wonderful about both seeing and hearing your words.

Each of those victories will give you the power to do more. Watch as those successes change your thinking and help you pursue your goals.

Coping with mental illness is a constant struggle. That's why you need to be constantly working on improving yourself. Seek out and find the positive wherever you can. Take the time to keep a success list and watch how it changes your life.

Day 14 | Love Yourself and Fight Bipolar

One of the hardest things to master when fighting mental illness is the ability to love yourself. Depression and anxiety seem to bring with them a sense of self-loathing. The darkness stifles most positive thoughts.

The thing is, self-love is also one of the most important things you must do to maintain mental stability. But how do you get there?

One way to learn to love yourself is to celebrate your wins. Take the time to recognize both your large and small accomplishments. More than just writing down the win, spend a few minutes celebrating it.

For example, reaching my first 500 email subscribers was a huge win for me. It was the culmination of three years of hard work. Most of that time, I was clueless about what I should be doing. The 500 milestone was a great day because I finally felt like I was getting the whole newsletter thing.

To celebrate my win, I took a night off, picked up my favorite dish from a local restaurant and a bottle of wine, and spent the night watching a movie I love. The party doesn't have to be big, but celebrating your win has value.

However, you don't achieve major milestones every day. There are days when all you can do is get dressed and feed yourself. Maybe with special mightiness, you can take a shower and wash the dishes. Success for the day might be just taking your meds or going to bed on time, but it's still a triumph.

Your celebration can also be small. Stand in front of the bathroom mirror, smile, and congratulate yourself. Say something like, "Hey, today was a tough day, but you beat it. You're still here, and that makes you a rockstar!"

The tiny wins are just as important as the monumental ones. Truth be told, I celebrate every email subscriber. It warms my heart deep inside to know people want to receive my writing. The win helps me continue to produce content.

If all you do today is keep yourself alive despite all the negative voices in your head, that's a win. Celebrate it. Pat yourself on the back, do a little dance, and enjoy the moment. You really are a rockstar.

Success breeds success, and the small wins turn into bigger ones. Learn to celebrate your wins, and you'll find the way to give yourself the love you deserve.

Journal Prompt: What are three wins you had in the past week? Which one means the most to you? Why?

Creative Writing Prompt: It's the championship game and everything hangs on your main character. Write a story about the game. Do they win?

Choose Words Carefully: Life Lessons From an Angry Book Review

Have you ever written a book? Talk to many people, and you will frequently hear, "write a book," is somewhere on their bucket list.

It's a worthwhile goal. Our world could benefit from more skilled writers. Whose life hasn't been changed by the words of a good book? Your life improved because the author took the time to choose their words carefully.

Book reviews are one of the most valuable things for an author. A good review will help grow an author's brand and inspire others to read their work. However, a bad review can be devastating.

What do book reviews have to do with living with a mental illness? We'll come back to that and why you should choose your words carefully. First, though, let's get a little backstory about what inspired this chapter.

A few years ago, I was trying to make a success of working from home. During part of my adventure, I partnered with an indie author and worked for a few months as his virtual assistant.

Those months taught me a lot about writing and why you should choose your words carefully. I was amazed at how much time and effort goes into getting that final manuscript together. Whether it's writing the first draft, the half-dozen edits it goes through, or the intense anxiety behind finally putting it out into the world, there's a lot of blood, sweat, and tears that go into the process.

When it was over, I felt like I had helped bring a child into that world. Now, I'm very protective of that child.

My time working with the author came to an end, but I still keep in touch and like to follow his progress. I'm always thrilled to jump on Goodreads or Amazon to see if there are any new reviews.

One day, I was overjoyed to find a fresh review. Things had been pretty quiet for a few weeks. I was thrilled to see a review consisting of more than just five words, as so many of them are.

What I read, though, made my blood boil.

First, it was a 1-Star review, which I find hard to understand in most cases. How genuinely awful does a book have to be to get a one-star rating?

I know how good this book is. I read it cover to cover at least three times.

Surely, I thought, *it had to be a mistake.*

But it got worse.

The reviewer, clearly a trained internet troll, went on a tirade about how the author had no talent, could not write a coherent story, and how the book was the worst story they ever read.

Part of me wonders if it's the only book they've ever read.

In any case, the reviewer clearly didn't even read the whole thing. They even disclosed later in their verbal bashing that they hadn't.

To an author, a finished book is like a precious baby. Months and years of time, energy, and tears are invested in the final product.

My rage boiled inside me the rest of the day. How could someone leave such a hateful review about a book they didn't even read? I wanted to find the person and smack them upside the back of their head.

Though I wanted to, I was apprehensive about reaching out to the author. I didn't want to be the one to ruin his day if he hadn't already seen the review.

Finally, a few nights later, I couldn't wait any longer. I dialed his number and began pouring out my fury as soon as he said, "Hello." In a few seconds, he was laughing, and I was utterly dumbfounded.

"How can you laugh?" I asked. "This person is saying your book is the worst book ever. Worst book *ever*!"

"Yes," he laughed at me. "And they won't be the last one. Bad reviews are part of being a writer."

I was in shock. As a writer myself, I was working on putting my first book together. Was this what I had to look forward to?

As I thought about the unkind words in the review, it had me doubting everything about my future goals. Could I endure being told that my book was the "worst book ever"?

"I'll tell you what," my author friend said. "Take a few minutes and go on Amazon and read the reviews for some of your favorite books. You'll see just how common this is."

Within minutes of getting off the phone, I had Amazon pulled up and began searching for books.

One of my all-time favorite books is *Sphere* by Michael Crichton, so I started there. I couldn't believe I found lots of 1-star reviews stating the book was:

- "Poorly written"
- "Boring and unimaginative"
- "A disappointing mess"
- "So bad that it actually hurt me to continue reading." *(Really?!)*

Okay, so science fiction is not for everyone. Maybe this one was a fluke.

Next, I decided to choose something more popular with the masses. My next victim was *The Notebook* by Nicholas Sparks. Everyone loves that book. Or so I thought.

I headed over to its page next. Of the more than 2,000 reviews on Amazon, there were dozens of one-star reviews. Dozens!

Here are some of the awful things that foolish people wrote about this iconic book.

- "So bad, I want my money back."
- "Void of all substance."
- "A very large letdown."
- "Worst romantic novel I've ever read."

And there were more pages filled with the same negativity.

For me, there are no words. I just don't get it.

Whenever I face a negative experience in my life, I try to discern if there is anything I can learn from it. Sitting down at the keyboard, I started pounding out my thoughts, good and bad. What I came up with were four reasons why you should choose your words carefully.

Here are a few lessons that came to mind.

1. Your Words Matter

IT'S PREVALENT IN TODAY'S world to throw words around with no thought. Even people in power are frequently degrading people in lower positions or of different races or nationalities.

Their defense, far too often, is that words don't matter.

They are 100 percent wrong.

Words do matter, and they matter a great deal. It's always necessary to choose your words carefully.

For instance, I don't know the person who left the terrible review of my friend's book. However, their cutting and downright mean words upset me for several days. Add to that, anyone else who goes to that book's page will now see their contempt for the book, and many will then choose not to give that excellent story a chance.

Every day we have a choice as to whether we will use our words to build someone up or tear them down. Choose wisely. The person you tear down today might be the person you need to build you up tomorrow.

2. Words Posted Online Hurt Real People

THE REVIEWER WHO LEFT the negative feedback may be a fine person. They might be a hardworking mom who was having a tough day or someone suffering from a toxic boss. I get that.

However, they forgot that their words were going to be read by a real person. If no one else reads a review, you can guarantee that the author, at least a new author, will read the words.

In the reviewer's haste to be degrading, they gave no thought to the emotional damage they were doing. I want to believe the best in people, so I want to think that wasn't their intent, but the damage is done.

Those of us with chronic illnesses probably spend more time online than healthy people. Being confined to home doesn't give us many other options to fill up our time.

It's essential that you choose your words carefully in terms of what words you are putting out there. Tearing someone down on social media is unacceptable, even if it's a celebrity. That person may be nothing more than a digital user name to you, but there's a real human on the other end. Choose your words carefully.

3. You Can Choose How You Will Respond

THE AUTHOR I WORKED with has a great attitude. If he read the review at all, he chose not to let it bother him. Some stranger was pouring out poison, but he decided not to drink it.

That's a lesson I'm trying to learn myself. Obviously, I'm still working on it.

You have the same choice every day. People will say hurtful things to and about you and your illness. You may not be able to stop the words, but you can choose how much power they have in your life.

4. Someone Will Always Be Negative

THE LAST LESSON IS a reminder to be realistic. We live in an angry world. Movies, music, and TV shows try to make us believe that attacking others with our words is the way to go.

Influenced by such a world, some people find their joy in destroying others. Knowing this, it's essential for you to prepare yourself.

People are going to say dumb things. They are going to be mean and degrading. If great authors like Michael Crichton and Nicholas Sparks aren't unscathed, then certainly everyday people like you and me should expect the same.

There is going to be someone who doesn't believe mental illness is a real illness. Some won't want to admit that you are chronically sick because you don't look like you're sick. That's okay. Forget them.

The only person that has to know the truth about you is *you*.

Own your truth and say goodbye to those who choose to be negative. If you respond at all, choose your words carefully. Surround yourself with positive people as much as possible. Don't be afraid to cut out of your life those who want to tear you down.

There's no way of knowing the true intent of the person who wrote my friend's review. If their goal was solely to damage my friend, well, I believe wholeheartedly that the universe will reward them for their kindness. On the positive side, the reviewer at least taught me how important it is to choose my words carefully.

If you can, please do one more thing this week. Take a moment to make an author's day. Browse Amazon or Goodreads for a book you've loved and write a review. It's another way to add more positivity to the world. If you haven't read a book recently, pick out a great one and read it.

You can choose your words carefully and decide to be better. I know all of you will make the right choice.

Go forth and heal yourself and the world with your carefully chosen words.

Day 15 | Ignore Your Mind When It Calls You Powerless

You are powerful.

If you're fighting a mental illness, you may be laughing right now. You might even think, "Scott, you crazy man. I can't even get my butt out of bed, and you're telling me I'm powerful? Seriously?"

Yes, seriously.

If you are alive and can communicate, you have the power of words. Carefully chosen words can build communities and conquer empires.

I can't help but think of Helen Keller. Both blind and deaf, Keller was truly cut off from the world around her. It's unfathomable to think about the pain and loneliness she felt before Anne Sullivan took the time to teach her how to communicate.

Keller was born in 1880, a time when having a disability made you an invisible part of society. Yet, she smashed the odds stacked against her.

In time, Keller became an American author, disability rights advocate, political activist, and lecturer. Her words still affect people today, myself included, over 50 years after her death.

You are just as powerful as Helen Keller, and you have so many more opportunities. Use your power.

Modern technology has made it possible for patients otherwise unable to communicate to still lead full lives. Stephen Hawking even guest starred on *The Big Bang Theory* long after he lost control of his body.

Hawking used his power to live as full a life as he could. And who wouldn't have loved to be part of that amazing show? You likely have many more chances to use your strength than he did.

Think today of your power. How can you use your words to build up others? What experiences do you have that could encourage someone else fighting the same battles?

You are powerful. Never forget that.

Journal Prompt: Who was your Anne Sullivan, the person to have the greatest impact on your life? How did they help you change? What lessons did you learn that you could teach others?

Creative Writing Prompt: Write a story about a day from Helen Keller's life. What did she feel? How did she perceive the world?

Be Inspired To Heal Your Broken Pieces

Do you ever feel broken? Does it ever seem like your life or illness has left you in pieces? Like Humpty Dumpty, are you thinking you'll never be whole again? Can you heal your broken pieces?

There's no doubt that living with a chronic illness can be crushing. Constant pain can cause insomnia, and too many nights without sleep will bring on madness, even if you don't have a mental disorder.

Take heart. You can put yourself together again.

Yes, those cracks may still show, but as you'll see in this chapter, your scars are part of what makes you beautiful. Let's talk a little more about the Japanese art of Kintsugi.

On Day 11, you read a little about Kintsugi. The word "Kintsugi" translates directly as "golden joinery." The art form consists of collecting broken pieces of pottery to make them whole again.

What makes Kintsugi so beautiful is what the artist uses to put the pieces back together. Most of the time it's gold, and those vibrant gold seams add a whole new level of artistic appeal to the once broken item.

For the pottery, what was once a fragmented item ready to be discarded now becomes an attractive piece of art.

When you're going to repair some broken pottery or a decorative plate, the first step is to gather all the pieces. To put yourself back together and heal your broken pieces, you want to start with the same step.

Since you don't literally have parts of you lying around the house, what does it mean to gather your pieces?

Start by taking an inventory of where you are right now. If your shattering blow was a mental illness diagnosis, your inventory may include reviewing what you already know about your condition and which questions you have that still need answers.

While you're taking inventory, be sure to note also how you are doing, both mentally and physically. Allow yourself to grieve over the event that broke you, and then try to come to terms with your new reality.

Acceptance is a vital tool in your recovery process. Recognizing where you are now and accepting your reality will go a long way in your recovery efforts.

When pottery is broken, there may be tiny pieces that can't be glued back together. Those fragments are then discarded and more gold is put in their place.

Yesterday is your tiny piece. Whatever happened, no matter what was said or done to you, there is nothing you can do to change yesterday. Nothing.

The scars of the past may always be with you. Even though they may heal, they may still leave a mark. And that's okay.

Those marks are your gold seams. Those scars are what makes you beautiful. They are proof of how you learned to heal your broken pieces.

Choose to focus on today and tomorrow, and yesterday will become less painful.

When a vessel is repaired using the Kintsugi method, it's usually not put back into use for its original purpose. A plate may never be used as a plate again. A vase may never hold water and flowers. However, that doesn't make the items useless.

Whatever illness you are now coping with, you are likely not the same as you were. There may be things you can no longer do or places you can no longer go. Those limitations do not define you.

As mentioned in the last chapter, Helen Keller and Stephen Hawking proved how it's possible to move forward despite limitations. With that in mind, take the time to learn what things you can do. Find new paths to travel, and new experiences to share. Life isn't over, so find new ways to live it.

Different is not necessarily bad. It's just different.

For a final comparison, consider the value of pottery that is put back together by Kintsugi. The original item may have had little value. The new piece, with its glittering gold stripes, is usually precious. In fact, many people collect these works of art.

In your case, think about how your struggles can help you and others. Is there someone you know who is going through a similar trial? Can you share your experiences to help prop them up? How can you use your pain to offer validation or acceptance to someone else?

Our challenges make us more valuable as people. Most of us gain more empathy, more kindness, and more understanding. Put those fresh insights to work by improving the lives of the people around you.

Building up others will help you heal your broken pieces.

I won't lie to you; I hate being sick. Really hate it. Waking up each day with trepidation about how my illnesses are going to dictate the day is frustrating and often makes me angry.

However, if it wasn't for the pain I've experienced, the bad times when bipolar knocked me down, I wouldn't be able to write this book. At the very least, it would be a much different book.

My pains, awful as there are, help me reach out to others and to show them how to endure trials. I want everyone to know life really can get better. Your experiences are just as valuable.

Think about how you can heal your broken pieces. Gather your fragments and start putting them back together again.

Remember the keys:

● Pursue acceptance

- Say goodbye to yesterday
- Recognize that things are different
- Help others

Even if it's just baby steps, do something to pour gold between your broken pieces. Let that precious metal solidify you and make you stronger. Then, spend a few moments with your journal and explore how far you've come.

Day 16 | Read Books to Improve Your Life

I love books. My mom filled me with a love for the written word by reading to me for many hours. Back when I was small enough to fit on her lap, I grabbed a book every time she was willing and begged her to read to me. Her attention helped me progress faster than many of my schoolmates.

E. B. White's *Charlotte's Web* was the first chapter book I read by myself. I sobbed like the child I was when I reached the end of the book. Once my tears dried, the impact of the experience hit me. Books were my first love.

During the decades since, hundreds of books meandered through my life. Many changed the way I see the world, but five special books affected me the most. Each one has a unique reason it made the list.

Pride & Prejudice by Jane Austen

PRIDE & PREJUDICE is one of the few books I have read more than once. The book is special to me both because it is a story of rich emotion but also because it was the particular favorite of my best friend, Lizzy, before she passed away. Every time I read it, I can still feel her presence within the pages.

Don't Sweat the Small Stuff by Richard Carlson

I'M NOT A FAN OF MOST self-help books, but *Don't Sweat the Small Stuff* is one worth reading. With 100 quick lessons, it taught me how to let go of many things. The book started me on my positivity path, one I now teach to others.

The Sphere by Michael Crichton

THE SPHERE made me a Michael Crichton fan. Introduced to me by a workmate, the book mesmerized me. Fear, anxiety, and fascination radiated through me as I flipped every page. I was under the sea with the doomed crew, feeling their concern as Crichton unfurled the tale. It introduced me to a more powerful form of writing, opening my eyes to what was possible. Once a fan, I read nearly all of Crichton's books.

The Artist's Way by Julia Cameron

A MUST READ FOR CREATIVES, *The Artist's Way* has brought me back to my love of writing several times. Julia Cameron teaches you how to be an artist while instilling the ability to love yourself. Even if you don't write or create art, this book will help you grow as a person.

Victims No Longer by Mike Lew

BEING A MALE SURVIVOR of childhood sexual abuse was a painful secret I didn't think anyone could understand. In the early 1990s, very few men were sharing their stories. Their silence made me think I had to conceal my past, too.

My therapist recommended *Victims No More*, and for the first time, I realized other men were fighting the same monsters. This book was instrumental in my coming to terms with my painful childhood.

Books are amazing gifts. They can transport you to fantasy worlds, open your heart, and refresh your hope. Take time every day to benefit from their bounty.

Think today about your favorite books. Why are they important to you? What lessons did they teach you? If you don't have a favorite, pick up a book and start reading today.

Journal Prompt: What is your favorite book? Why? How did reading it change your life?

Creative Writing Prompt: Pick a character from your favorite book and write a story about the best day of their life. Bonus points if you can include yourself in the story.

Learn To Embrace the Bad Days

Today has been a bad day. It follows a string of terrible days. Both my Familial Mediterranean Fever (FMF) and my bipolar disorder joined forces and ganged up on me. Coping is difficult.

I am miserable.

Feeling so rough, it's almost impossible to write. The longer I stay in bed, though, the more valuable I think this chapter might be. So here goes.

Before I begin, I want to specify what type of nasty days I'm talking about.

Specifically, I'm referring to the days that come after a period of successfully coping with your mental illness. The days that sweep you off your feet and kick you in the head. The ones that won't let you forget you have an illness or that it will always be with you.

These are the days my mom always called, "Milk and cookies, pull the blankets up over your head days."

Personally, I prefer Barq's Root Beer and Krispy Kreme doughnuts, but that's a story for another time.

Can you cope with awful days when they arrive like a well-placed gut punch? Is there a way to survive the mental anguish and darkness that comes with them?

I believe there is, and this chapter will give you a few coping mechanisms.

All too frequently over the years, I have seen friends and family members stop taking their medication because of a string of dreadful days. The negative experience, in their minds, was proof their meds had stopped working.

Typically, that's not true.

A painful fact is that we all have bad days. Whether you have perfect health or teeter on the edge of insanity, there will be terrible days in your life.

Even the best drug cocktail or natural treatment plan cannot make every day all rainbows and butterflies. It will never happen. A bad day doesn't mean your therapy stopped working. Often, it's just a bad day, and everyone has them.

Knowing the truth, start evaluating your harder days by taking an honest evaluation of the situation. How long has this bad spell lasted? What were things like before they turned dark? Is there anything you did to bring on the event?

Taking a moment to acknowledge that there will be bad days, and learning to expect and accept them, will go a long way to help you cope with them. Here are a few more things you can do.

The first thing you'll want to do is find the place you will be most comfortable. Maybe you like to take long baths, sprawl out in bed, or have a favorite spot on the couch.

Go to your place, and give yourself permission to be there.

Do something nice for yourself at the same time. Make a cup of herbal tea, grab the heating pad or ice pack, get your softest blanket, and go curl up.

Often, the fastest way out of a string of bad days is to take some time to rest and recharge. So take the time you need.

Next, find some healthy distractions. Pull out a book you've been meaning to read, catch up on the show you've been too busy to watch, or pull up a movie online.

I'm a bit of a TV junkie. I love television series and follow way too many of them. My online watchlist has hundreds of things queued up, so it's easy to find a video to watch. When life feels like a dumpster fire, I give myself permission to watch episodes all day.

Binge watching shows is a great way for me to get out of my head and to stop thinking about how much pain I'm in.

Find a healthy escape that works for you.

It's already a bad day, so throw your diet or exercise routine out the window. Just for today, mind you, not forever.

Allow yourself to have a bowl of rocky road ice cream, chocolate chip cookie dough, or buttery pasta. Today is a bad day, and you deserve comfort food to help you cope with the tough times.

Moderation is key. If you eat two tubes of cookie dough, you'll hate yourself tomorrow. But it's okay to allow yourself some sort of treat.

Next, turn on some music that makes you feel calm or invokes happy memories. Light your favorite scented candle or open the windows to let in some fresh air.

Today is about taking care of you.

There is a lot to be said for sticking to a sleep routine. It's essential for keeping mental illness at bay.

Usually, I preach the value of getting up at the same time every day and will tell you to get your butt out of bed because beds should only be for sleeping.

For today, though, since it's a bad day, sleep as long as you want. Stay in bed. Pull the blankets up over your head. Today is your day to heal what hurts inside.

There's one more thing to do to have a successful bad day.

You gave yourself permission to lounge and snack and sleep all day today. That's fine, but tomorrow has to be better.

Now, I know what you're thinking. Tomorrow might not be any better. You may be right.

As I said, when I wrote this, I was in the middle of an FMF attack. An attack comes with a high fever, body aches from head to toe, and the never-ending spin that feels like I've just stepped off of a high-speed merry-go-round.

FMF attacks usually last 2-3 days, so I know the end will come. As I lay there enjoying the best the internet offers, I promise myself I will get up and back to work as soon as the fever breaks.

What does all this mean for your tomorrow?

As soon as you can, get up at your usual time. Brush your teeth, take a shower, and put on clothes for going out in public. Even if you still feel too bad to return to your other daily duties, take these steps.

Why?

Because giving in to the hard days can become a habit. It's too easy to stay in bed every day, eat all the wrong things, and never exercise. During an awful crash in 1996, I spent nearly three months in bed. It's not a healthy way to cope long term and caused me more harm than good.

So now, I try to only give myself one day to stay in bed. Then, I decide the next day will be better.

If your bipolar or another chronic illness causes a bad day, accept it. Own the day, and allow yourself all the luxuries you should have on a bad day.

The catch is, you only get one day. Whatever you have to do, make tomorrow better, even if it's only by a little bit.

You have it in you to get up and fight again. You will survive this bad day as you have so many others. I have faith in you and know you can do it.

Day 17 | See What Happens When You Try

Potential is a marvelous thing. In the frame of a second, anything is possible. The tiniest moment can change your life.

Every time I publish a post online or send out an email newsletter, I think about potential. My creation could be a viral hit or an epic fail. Millions may open and read it or I may sleep softly to the sound of crickets. There's no way to know for sure, but the potential is always there.

On Monday nights, I check my stats on various sites. I'm always most interested in my open rate for my email newsletter. Each time I click that button to go to the stats page, part of me expects the open rate to be at zero.

Happily, that has never happened. Some weeks, the open rate is as high as 65 percent. My worry is usually for nothing.

It's easy to forget about potential when you have a mental illness. The tendency is to fixate on your limitations rather than on the things you can still do. What would happen if you thought of the possibilities?

I never thought I could run a successful blog or publish a book, but the blog has been running since 2018 and you're reading this book. The possibilities can become reality. Dreams come true. I considered the potential and moved forward despite my doubts.

Every success gives you the power to try new things. Each goal achieved helps you see new possibilities.

Think about the potential in your life. What things can you still do? What seems beyond your reach but may still be possible? If you never try, you'll never know what you can do. Take a step today.

Journal Prompt: What is one thing you never thought you could do but ultimately accomplished? Is there a lesson you can learn from the experience? What do you want to try next?

Creative Writing Prompt: Write a story about a young girl who discovers she can fly. Does she tell anyone? How does she use her power?

Choose To See the Flower Not the Thorns

There's a popular meme on social media with the words, "Gratitude won't fix your mental illness."

It's a true statement, but the meme makes people think gratitude is unimportant. In reality, practicing gratitude is one of the most helpful things you can do to maintain your mental health.

A chemical imbalance in the brain often causes mental illness. No amount of positive thinking is going to fix the imbalance. However, the goal of being grateful isn't to fix your mental disorder. Instead, gratitude is about improving your mindset.

When you adjust what you're focusing on, your entire life changes.

It may sound like an oversimplification, but I promise you, it's true. Some people see the beautiful, fragrant rose, while others only see the thorns. It's the same bush, but focus affects everything. Gratitude is how you shift your focus.

When I chose to see the flower, my life improved. Let me explain.

When you have a mental illness, it can become your entire identity. After my bipolar disorder diagnosis, many of my friends only saw the broken part of me. They knew my poor choices led to a hospital stay. Many of them felt they had to discuss my mental health every time they saw me. While their intentions were good, the constant focus on my mental illness overwhelmed me.

As my friends focused on my illness, I decided I wanted to be something more. I chose things that mattered to me and got busy.

I pursued my writing and worked on strengthening my faith. When I saw friends, I talked about the positive things I was doing or encouraging things I'd read and limited conversation about my illness.

Many days, I felt truly awful inside, but my change in focus gave me an anchor. I no longer had to hide from conversations because I had topics I wanted to discuss. Just like I could choose where to focus, I also found I could steer conversations to better shores.

It took some time, but, as my conversations changed, so did the way I felt. My shift in focus improved my mindset. With a better attitude, I started to live up to what I was pursuing.

I applied the lesson to other parts of my life and learned to practice mindfulness and daily gratitude. In time, I started a gratitude jar. It became a tangible place where I could see how many blessings were all around me.

As I focused on the positive things, my life improved. Choosing to see the flowers made me see more of the beautiful things in the world. Now, most days, I can talk about anything and it doesn't bring me down. My illness no longer weighs me down because I proved to myself that I am so much more.

The words you say matter. So does your mindset. Where you choose to focus can either make your life positive or negative. I choose positive.

Choose to see the flowers. Choose Joy. Practice gratitude.

Day 18 | Forgive Yourself and Heal

"**I** forgive you."

Those three words may be some of the most powerful in the world. Some say forgiveness is a gift you give yourself and the other person.

While forgiving others is important, today we're going to focus on self-forgiveness. If you're battling a mental illness, such as bipolar disorder, you likely spend some time beating yourself up. I know I do.

I spend many of my nights awake, staring into the darkness, reliving all of my worst mistakes. I remember every horrible thing I've ever said and all the nasty things I've done. And there's more than enough replay clips to last the whole night. Most of my loved ones forgave me for the awful things I did decades ago, but I still hold them against myself.

When you're learning to live with a mental illness, your world can change from day to day. A task you could do yesterday may feel impossible today. The medication that worked last week can change overnight to one no more effective than popping peanut M&M's.

Since you know every day can be unique, you constantly have to look for better ways to manage your illness. Part of that includes continuing to try new things, and not all of them will be successful.

When you mess up, take some time to forgive yourself. Acknowledge any pain you caused, but do your best to move forward. Staying stuck in a moment of failure accomplishes nothing. Instead, it leads to increased stress levels and sleepless nights, and I'm already staying awake enough for both of us.

"To err is human," the old saying begins. You are human, so you're going to mess up. It's that simple. Until you're perfect, you have to forgive your own imperfections.

For today, focus on forgiveness. Take a few minutes to write an answer for today's journal prompt. Forgiving yourself will help keep you on the path to positivity.

Journal Prompt: What is one thing you haven't forgiven yourself for? Write a letter to yourself offering forgiveness.

Creative Writing Prompt: After years of self-loathing, a woman learns to forgive herself. Write a story about the reason she needed forgiveness. How did she finally find peace?

Practice Forgiveness by Asking, "Was the Sin Worthy of a Life Sentence?"

As each year comes to a close, most of us think about the prior year and what things we want to do differently in the new year. One thing we should add to our list is forgiveness.

Have you ever made a mistake? Committed a sin? Have your careless words or actions hurt someone?

I'm sure you're answering, "Yes." We are all sinners, falling short of perfection. It's the definition of being human. We mess up no matter how hard we try to do the right things. Our mistakes hurt others and cause problems. It's part of the messiness of life.

If we're all the same, why is forgiveness so hard? Maybe the problem is how we look at the mistake.

How would you feel if you received a life sentence? It's a scary thought. To know one mistake, one bad action, could predetermine the rest of your days, is terrifying. Most of us do our best to be law-abiding citizens, so we never have to worry about such a fate.

As awful as it would be to receive a life sentence, we don't think twice about handing them out.

Wait, what? I'm not a judge, you're probably thinking. *How am I handing out life sentences?*

By failing to forgive.

You get a thorn in your side because someone hurt you, and you refuse to pluck it out. You may carry the pain for years–sometimes for a lifetime–refusing to forgive the person who hurt you.

Life sentence. The words freeze me in my tracks when I think about them. Would I want my mistake to cost me a life sentence? Would you?

How many times have you held on to a grudge or refused to forgive someone? I'm more guilty than I would like to admit. When you refuse to release your resentment, you are placing a life sentence on the erring party.

Life sentences in the criminal justice system are only issued for the worst crimes. You have to be a wicked person and have done horrific things before warranting such a severe punishment.

Is there really any "sin" against you that is worth such a harsh punishment? Is the mistake stuck in your craw deserving of a lifetime of penance?

It's a powerful thought.

Most of the things we hold on to are nowhere near as serious as the worst crimes featured on the news. Even so, we're often inclined to hold on to the pain a friend caused us.

Is the punishment equal to the transgression?

Stealing a cookie is not even on the same planet as killing someone. Obviously, the punishment for each crime should be vastly different.

With hurt feelings, though, we may respond to all failings the same way.

- You hurt me, so I'm cutting you out of my life.
- You didn't invite me for dinner, so I'm not speaking to you.
- You shared my secrets, so I will never tell you anything again.

Does that seem like a fair punishment to you?

This is all well and wonderful in theory. It makes perfect sense that the punishment for a sin should fit the crime. It's the basis of most justice systems.

When the pain is in your heart, the misdeed feels much bigger. How do you learn to repeal the life sentences your heart demanded?

One way is the time test. Will the thing that happened matter in a year? Five years? 100 years? If not, can you let it go now? Cancel the life sentence.

Another solution is to think about your own mistakes. Who was the last person you hurt? Was it intentional? More often than not, it was probably just a careless moment. Do you want it held against you for the next five or ten years? Of course not.

When you think about how you want others to forgive you, it will help you be more forgiving.

I'll admit, I struggle with my internal justice system. Bipolar disorder often makes me think in black and white. Either you're in my life or out of it forever. I know that's unbalanced, and it's something I'm constantly working on improving.

When you know how easily you might issue a life sentence, it's time to reconsider the ones handed out. Do any of those people warrant parole?

Trust me, I know how tough this one is. It's easy to get stuck in a moment when you're hurt, or even worse, when someone you love is harmed. Repealing life sentences takes time and effort, and you won't make it from zero to 60 overnight.

It's okay to start small. Spend some time working on your own prison reform. Can you commute some life sentences or reduce the severity of other punishments you've handed out?

Part of pursuing a positive mindset includes letting go of the past. It's worth the effort to learn to forgive. It's time to move forward.

Have you been handing out life sentences when friends hurt you? Then now is the time to make changes and set those people free.

Day 19 | Do Acts of Kindness to Help You Move Past Your Grief

It was a Tuesday in July 2007 when I lost my best friend.

We were both at work and had a brief telephone conversation about how stupid one of our friends was acting. Neither of us had much time, so we said only a few words. We made plans for dinner and each hung up.

Less than an hour later, she was gone. Losing her was the worst experience of my life.

The act of grieving is a slow process, and the worst of it often comes in waves. During the worst days, I learned a valuable lesson about how to cope with grief and the toughest days life throws at you.

One of the best ways to wrestle with your emptiness and pain is to get busy doing acts of kindness for those in need. The ache inside doesn't go away completely, but having a purposeful task to concentrate on relieves some of the internal downward spiral.

For me, I've always enjoyed reading to older adults. One of the finest gifts God gave me was the ability to read well. In the last 30 years, I've spent thousands of hours reading to those who struggled to read for themselves.

When my grief was the hardest to face, I got busy again. I looked for ways to help others, and I did what I could.

If you have a mental illness, there are days you're limited in what you can do. Except for the worst days, I could usually still read. So I visited my older friends, let them select the book, and dedicated more time to making their lives a little better.

A marvelous gift happened along the way. Several of my older friends knew the pain I was suffering as they had lived through similar grief. I read to them, and they shared their wisdom. I'm not sure I could have gotten through the hardest of those days without them.

For today, think of a kind act you can do for someone else. It can be as simple as sending a card or even a text message. Find one person today who needs your encouragement, and shower them with all the time and attention you can.

Journal Prompt: Make a list of people you know who could use your help. What could you do to make their lives better? What's the kindest thing that's ever been done for you? How did it make you feel?

Creative Writing Prompt: An older man is surprised when a group of teens show up at his house to attend to some long-overdue chores. At the end of the day, to express his appreciation, he tells them a story. Write that story.

Appreciate the Value of Trials By Fire

What was your last serious trial? What did you learn from it? Is there a way to appreciate the value of a trial by fire?

If you're coping with bipolar disorder, you may feel many of your struggles lead one right into the next. Even if that's true, is there anything positive to be gained from trials?

This chapter will teach you a lesson from the Jack Pine tree. For this tree, a trial by fire is a necessity. You may find that, at some point, a fire was equally important in your life.

Jack Pines are a species of coniferous tree that grows in the forests of Canada and the midwest and northeast in the United States. The trees are also called scrub pines or gray pines and stand out as unique among pine trees.

While most pines develop pinecones that open over time, releasing their seeds, the Jack Pine produces a cone with a tight resin seal. Rain, weather, and time do not by themselves remove this wax covering. The tree's only hope of reproducing is under lock and key.

These unique pinecones are not indestructible. Rather, they just need a little encouragement to release their precious cargo. That nudge must be a temperature equal to or greater than 122° F (50° C). Most often, this help comes as a literal trial by fire.

The best type of fire is not the raging destructive type frequently highlighted on the news. Instead, these trees need a low burning flame that stays close to the ground and never reaches the tree's canopy. This burn is hot enough to release the cone's seeds without doing serious damage to the trees or forest.

You are like the sealed cone of the Jack Pine. No, you don't need intense heat to reproduce, but the flames in your life often reveal what you can do. Those new insights are your gifts.

Usually, you can't see these gifts during a serious trial. Just like literal fire can be terrifying, the trials you face in life often are as well.

Living with multiple illnesses, I often feel like I'm being thrown from one burning flame to the next. One of the worst trials–like flames nipping at my heels–is anxiety. It's my daily companion. The internal turmoil makes leaving the house, being in public, and driving a challenge every day.

Some months ago, I asked my doctor if there was anything we could do to improve things. I don't have the luxury of not working. Eating is important, and I can't afford food if I stay home. So, leaving the house and driving are daily necessities. Add to that, I drive for my aged parents a few times a week.

My doctor recommended I try a new medicine. Short story, it was a terrible idea. I mean the "staying awake for days with anxiety so bad you can't close your eyes" kind of awful.

As I look back now, I can see the seeds released by my trial.

When a fire sweeps through a forest, even one of these healthy burns, things will look drastically different afterward. Health, money, and relationship trials might scorch your figurative earth and make you feel like you're in a foreign land once it's passed.

That's how I felt. Amid the worst of the increased anxiety brought on by the medication, I felt like things were constantly spinning and slightly blurred. When I finally started to feel more like my normal self, my world was an alien landscape.

In reality, nothing changed, at least not on the outside. Instead, my perception of things was different.

My life couldn't stop when things were at their worst, so I found a way to push myself forward to do most of the things expected of me. I missed more than a few social events and several days of work, but I kept going.

Knowing what I did to keep going now makes it obvious when others around me are struggling, especially if they are coping with anxiety.

I never bought into the whole empath-thing in the past, but now, I can't help but wonder if there is some truth to it. There are times I walk into a room, and everyone in the room will be laughing, but my attention immediately goes to one person. In an instant, I can feel their anxiety and turmoil.

Now, I see the world with fresh eyes.

When the fire in the forest burns out, the seeds of the Jack Pine are hard to find. They are there, in the burned soil, ready to start a new life, but you have to look for them.

Likewise, when the worst of your trial lets up, it may take some looking to see what lessons you've gained.

Maybe you've gained a new sense of empathy. There could be a friend you grew closer to during the ordeal or learned to see from a new perspective. Sometimes your seed is a sense of calm gained from understanding how a terrible thing happened, but you survived it.

Whatever it might be, if you look for it, you will find a seed that makes your world a bit better.

The Jack Pine cone will release its seed in one other circumstance: intense cold. Temperatures that drop to −51° F (−46° C) will cause the cone's wax to become brittle and break, thus releasing the seeds.

Similarly, not all trials look the same. Just because you don't see flames doesn't mean you're not in the midst of one.

In the days to come, make sure you take a few moments to think things over. Look for subtle differences in the way you feel or act or the things you notice in others. Watch how your heart and mind respond when you talk with loved ones and reflect on any changes.

With a little contemplative thought, you will find gifts, small seeds released by your trial.

As the old adage goes, "What doesn't kill you makes you stronger." Recognize the strengths you've gained and celebrate your victory. Surviving a trial by fire is a great win, so make a note of it.

Day 20 | Say Goodbye to the Past

When you're diagnosed with a mental illness, you experience a sort of death. In the seconds it takes a doctor to say the words, your entire life changes.

I experienced this death in the mid-1990s when I was first diagnosed with bipolar disorder and then again in 2016 when an internist diagnosed me with Familial Mediterranean Fever.

Nothing really changed with either statement, but my universe shifted.

The hard reality is living with illness changes your life. Some things you wanted to achieve will now be impossible. It's easy to slip into a state of total despair. You may become so fixated on the life you wanted that you're unable to see any future possibilities.

If that's where you are, it's time to stop looking back. You're still a breathing human being, so your life isn't over. Your goals may have to change, but your ability to lead a full life is still there.

To move forward, look for the possibilities in your world.

My bipolar diagnosis sent me into a tailspin because I wrapped many of my dreams around the idea of being healthy. I imagined that being tied to medication for the rest of my life would make everything I hoped for unattainable.

My life didn't end in 1995. I didn't even start my blog until 2018, and the real growth of my online content only began in 2021. Saying goodbye to my past dreams has enabled me to create new goals and move in directions I never imagined.

I hate bipolar disorder. It touches every part of my life and distorts much of my world, but it's also helped me see the world differently. The life lessons I've learned from having a mental illness keep me writing. I hope my words will improve the lives of others.

For today, pick something from your past and say goodbye to it. Maybe it's a relationship, a home, a career, or maybe just a thought process. Give yourself permission to move on and then look to the future.

Your life is not over, but you can't move forward as long as you're looking backwards. Say goodbye and step forward.

Journal Prompt: Write a letter to say goodbye to something from your past. Explain why you need to say farewell and how you're going to move ahead. Pick a goal you want to focus on for your future.

Creative Writing Prompt: Write a story about a woman who wakes up one morning with no memory of her past life. Does she try to get her memory back or move forward with a new life?

Find the Inspiration You Need To Never Give Up

Any hope for survival seemed impossible. The team of 28 men had been away for over 400 days in one of the most inhospitable environments in the world. Their trip to explore the wonders of Antarctica was one they feared they would not survive.

Fortunately for those men, they had an amazing captain who knew the key to survival was keeping hope and determination alive. If you can hang on to your hope, then that driving force can lead you to survival and success.

In today's turbulent world, the desire is strong to just give up. You may feel like you're living in a similar inhospitable land with no hope of getting out alive. Yet, history has proved we can overcome even the most insurmountable of obstacles.

Consider how Sir Ernest Shackleton's journey and a shipwreck 100 years ago can help you face your challenges in today's world.

Born on February 15, 1874, in county Kildare, Ireland, Ernest Henry Shackleton lived in a very different world than today. Raised in London, the second of 10 children, Shackleton was always an adventurer.

His father envisioned a medical career for him, but Ernest's calling was to be an explorer. At age 16, he joined the merchant navy. He achieved the rank of a first mate by the time he was 18. Within six years, he became a certified master mariner.

Shackleton's great white whale was his determination to conquer the South Pole. In 1901, accompanying Robert Falcon Scott on his first venture to the South Pole, they reached a point closer than anyone else had ever made it. The trip was arduous and left Shackleton with a serious illness that sent him back home. In 1907, he made a second attempt and reached within 97 miles of his destination before the fierce cold and wind forced him to turn back.

Another explorer, Roald Amundsen, stole his victory by becoming the first man to step foot on the South Pole in 1911. Part of his dream crushed, Shackleton was not one to give up. He was intent on finishing his own expedition to the region.

So it was on August 1, 1914, Shackleton shipped out from London on the ship Endurance for his third trip to the South Pole. Little did he know how prophetic his ship's name would become.

Within a few months, the mariners reached the small island of South Georgia in the southern Atlantic. On December 5, the adventurers began the final leg of their journey. It was a trip that would keep them away from dry land for the next 497 days.

In early January 1915, the Endurance became trapped in ice. As ships were less robust in days past, Shackleton made the tough decision to abandon his ship. The men set up camp on a floating ice sheet nearby.

Later in 1915, the men watched as their ship was slowly crushed and devoured by the angry sea. By April 1916, Shackleton knew they had to do something if they were to survive. With their three remaining small boats, they set off for Elephant Island, which is near the tip of Cape Horn.

Elephant Island was no sanctuary. The island was uninhabited and far from any normal shipping routes. Any hope of being rescued meant they had to get off Elephant Island to a place where there were people.

Shackleton knew time was running out for him and his men. Worn out physically and emotionally, he chose five of his crew to travel with him in a 22-foot lifeboat. Their aim was to make it back to a whaling station on South Georgia Island. Fierce sea conditions forced them to land the boat 20 miles from the desired station.

With no climbing equipment, sub-zero temperatures, and winds bombarding them, his small party trekked an uncharted path through snow-covered mountains to reach the station. From there, he could finally lead a rescue party back to collect the rest of his crew. It took another 17 days.

The most amazing part of Shackleton's journey is that all 28 of his men made it home again. They lost no one. Even though survival seemed impossible, Shackleton's staunch determination and optimism kept his men from giving up.

Asked later what helped his crew keep going despite seemingly hopeless odds, each sailor replied that they believed their captain would keep his word and rescue them. Shackleton knew in his mind he would rescue his men, and his confidence became the lifeblood of everyone with him.

Like Shackleton, you are living in challenging times. Maybe you're not lost on a frozen sheet of ice, but you're likely facing some tough situations. You may even doubt the possibility of your survival.

Now is not the time to give up. If you feel you are close to the breaking point, consider how these seven lessons can help you keep going.

1. Focus On The Light

A LIGHT SHINES ITS brightest when everything around it is dark. When your world goes dark, you may become consumed by the darkness, focusing on it to the point you are oblivious to any light.

Light is always there. Maybe it's just a speck in the distance, but it is there.

It's imperative you look for the light. If you can find even a hint of illumination, point all your attention towards it.

It's too easy to close your eyes when life gets hard. Pain and fear can trick you into thinking you can't bear anything else. Keeping your eyes closed, like a child at a scary movie, seems to be the safest course to follow.

Fight the urge and open your eyes.

Living with mental illness, I am no stranger to the darkness. Bipolar depression can coat my world with black tar. The chaos of today's world only adds to my burden, but I refuse to keep my eyes closed.

Think about this: you have already survived every bad thing that's happened to you.

Every. Single. Thing.

That means you have a 100 percent success ratio for dealing with life's trials. There's a bit of light.

Your current difficulties might be greater than any of the past, but, as my mother always says, "Where there's life, there's hope." Shackleton taught his men the same lesson.

Hope is the light you need to find.

Have you ever watched a sunrise or been awake during the darkest hours of morning?

The first hints of sunlight are barely discernible. As the minutes pass, something magical happens as the light slowly infiltrates the sky.

Keep looking for the light, and you will find it.

2. It's Okay To Start Over

YOUR CURRENT STRUGGLES may have you feeling terrified right now. Maybe you lost a job or closed a business. You may be coping with the end of a long-term relationship or bouncing back from an addiction relapse. Just because something ends doesn't mean you do.

I have failed at three businesses. That's a painful truth. I share this tidbit so you know where I'm coming from. The first thing to know is failure is rarely fatal.

When everything crumbles, you can't help but try to put things back together. Yet, sometimes, you can't put Humpty Dumpty back together again. That's okay. Maybe he shouldn't be what he was.

Relationships, businesses, and creative endeavors may all fail. It may even be an epic fail. My last business venture left me with no profits and about $17,000 in debt.

Whatever your situation, ask yourself, "What can I learn from this?"

Many times, the trial is not a complete failure. What may at first seem to be a loss may prove to be a milestone on the road to a better success.

Thomas Edison is rumored to have said, "I have not failed 10,000 times. I have not failed once. I have succeeded in proving that those 10,000 ways will not work. When I have eliminated the ways that will not work, I will find the way that will work."

Learn from today and start new tomorrow.

3. Things Will Get Better

DURING A CRISIS, IT'S hard to imagine a better future. Even so, every storm, no matter how severe, eventually passes.

What will the world look like after this trial? It's hard to say, but uncertainty doesn't have to spell doom. Shackleton's men must have shuddered with terror, sleeping night after night on a sheet of ice. Yet, their rescue and better times came, and yours will, too.

Imagine a better world, and let it keep you going.

4. Do the Impossible

THINK ABOUT THE PRECEDING Thomas Edison quote. At one time, cell phones, the internet, and computers were all impossibilities. No doubt many people said, "There's no way that could ever be done."

Fast forward to today, and those things are not only possible, but vital to our livelihoods. People can do more with the processing power of a smartphone than the first computer manufacturers could even envision.

Impossible is a mindset and a limiting belief. Throw it out, and hope and optimism will return.

Before his voyage, everyone thought a journey like Shackleton's was impossible. No doubt there were times his men felt the same. Shackleton himself may have even had self-doubt in his heart.

Doubt or not, those men refused to give up until they could prove they could do the impossible. You will conquer today's impossibilities as well.

Remind yourself that nothing is impossible.

5. Keep Trying

SHACKLETON SET THE standard in refusing to give up. Imagine being stuck on an island of ice. Temperatures may have been colder than they'd ever felt, and there was no way of communicating with anyone outside their party.

If ever there was a time to feel hopeless, that would have been it.

Shackleton felt he had to keep trying. He wanted his men to survive and make it back to their families, and the best way to do that was for all of them to keep trying.

When you're experiencing dark days, hope is hard to come by, but you must keep going.

Polio, tuberculosis, and the plague were all hopeless causes, but through science and ingenuity, each of those conditions can now be controlled. You never know what the future will bring, but you have to stay here if you're going to see it. You must keep living.

6. Go Slow

TREKKING OVER A MOUNTAIN in the Antarctic region had to be a slow journey. Between wind and cold and the fatigue brought on by a malnourished team, there must have been many moments they wanted to just lie down in the snow and go to sleep.

Their insistence to keep moving made survival possible. One foot in front of the other, they all made it home.

Your life might be in ruins, but it won't always be. Take the little you have and find a way to move forward. Forward is forward, even if it's baby steps.

Go slow if you have to, but keep going.

7. Never Give Up

I'D LOVE TO SAY MY life is all rainbows and butterflies, but that would be a colossal lie. Living every day with a chronic illness and a brain that's my own worst enemy is overwhelming on a good day. The insanity of today's world shrouded in fear every time you leave your home is taking its toll.

Insomnia is often an issue, and my mind races constantly. Most days, it feels like my heart never stops racing.

What keeps me going? The seven things mentioned above. Let's review.

1. Keep looking for the light.
2. Learn from today and start new tomorrow.
3. Imagine a better world.
4. Remind yourself that nothing is impossible.
5. Always keep trying.
6. Go slow if you have to, but never stop.
7. Never give up.

The phrases, "Never give up," and, "Keep fighting," are my mantras. I may face tough days, but experience has taught me things will get better again.

Shackleton and his men never wavered in their determination to get back home. You must continue to fight with the same tenacity. After all, your struggles have likely lasted nowhere near the 497 days his crew endured.

Hold on to your loved ones and remember, you're not alone. By continuing to support each other, you can keep hope alive. You will conquer and come out stronger on the other side.

Day 21 | Use Belief to Help You Cope With Mental Illness

Belief is a powerful tool. In one of my favorite movies, *Hook*, Peter Banning (Robin Williams) is really Peter Pan, but he forgot his past. It's only when he started to believe again that everything in his world changed.

You don't have the option of living in Neverland, but there is a lesson you can learn from Peter. Positive thinking affects your world and your health.

In fact, some studies show that people with a family history and high-risk factors for coronary artery disease were 13 percent less likely to have a heart attack or other coronary event if they had a positive mindset.

I don't know about you, but I'll take a 13 percent gain every day of the week. There are not a lot of positive odds in the life of the chronically ill, so you have to take every advantage you can get.

Believing you will survive improves your chances of success, whether you're lost in the wilderness or battling a mental illness.

It's easy to forget the power of belief when you're sick every day. The constant aches and pains, the chorus of negative voices in your head, and the crushing weight of depression can make it near impossible to believe things will ever get better.

Think of this: How long was your worst day? It might have felt longer, but it was only 24 hours. And you survived it. Imagine what else you can do.

The worst days always end. It may take finding a new treatment or adjusting the dosages of your current meds, but better days are possible. Belief is the power to keep you afloat during the hardest days. Be like Peter and believe.

For today, imagine your life without the problems weighing you down. Think about a time when anxiety won't keep you confined at home or when physical exhaustion won't equate to being in bed for days. If you believe a better life is possible, you may achieve it.

No, belief won't cure your illness, but it can make it more endurable. Hold on to the hope that better days will come and they will.

Journal Prompt: Imagine you wake up tomorrow in perfect health in a world without problems. Describe your day.

Creative Writing Prompt: Like Peter in *Hook*, you find out you are a famous character from a children's book or movie. Who are you? How do you find out? What do you do once you know?

Turn Your Obstacles Into Stepping Stones

Have you heard about the blind mountain climber? No, this isn't the opening line of a joke. Instead, it's a story about how to overcome obstacles.

Can you imagine climbing a mountain if you were blind? Where would you even begin your journey?

That's precisely what Erik Weihenmayer did. He is one of only 150 climbers to conquer the Seven Summits, which includes Mount Everest.

As you consider his story, think about how you can overcome the obstacles in your life.

Climbing a mountain wasn't the first obstacle that Weihenmayer had to face. He was not born blind, but he lost his sight by his early teens from a condition known as retinoschisis.

Blind or not, Weihenmayer refused to be limited by his circumstances. His goal was to be a teacher and blindness would not stop him.

However, the limiting beliefs of others almost stopped him in his tracks. Many people didn't believe a blind man could successfully teach. How would he be able to help his students without being able to see where they needed help? Would he be able to keep a room full of teenagers from erupting into chaos if he couldn't see their actions?

Happily, in time, a few people believed in Weihenmayer and worked to give him the chance to prove what type of teacher he could be.

The result? Weihenmayer became not only a successful and effective teacher but one of the most beloved educators in the school system.

Another obstacle in his life had been conquered, and Weihenmayer was intent on tackling more. His belief set moved him to conquer all seven of the summits mentioned earlier.

How about you? What is your obstacle? What stands in your way to achieving the life you want to have?

Perhaps, like me, you are living with mental illness. You may think that just staying alive each day takes all of the energy you have to give.

I get it. I've been there often. Rarely are the awful days unending. Better days come, and it's up to you to make the best use of them.

Like Weihenmayer, I have chosen to keep pressing forward. Every day, I work to overcome my obstacles. You can do the same.

One of the biggest keys to success in Weihenmayer's story is his mindset. No matter what was thrown at him, he never viewed it as an insurmountable wall.

To be honest, I can barely imagine walking to the bathroom without sight. The thought of climbing a mountain while not being able to see would terrify me.

Weihenmayer didn't do it on his own, though. He had a goal he wanted to achieve and was willing to ask for help to get there.

What about you? Who in your life can help you reach your goals? Are you willing to ask for help? Why do some people succeed where others have failed? Often, it is just a matter of continuing on, refusing to quit. Overcoming obstacles requires tenacity.

Would you keep going if you knew that this hurdle was going to be your last?

Everyone faces challenges and difficult situations. It's a painful fact of life. Refusing to quit, though, is what separates success from failure.

When dealing with mental health issues, this may mean seeking out a new treatment or doctor. It could require trying a different medication or combination of drugs.

Obviously, the application here isn't to go do something beyond your means. Living with an illness is a constant balancing act.

As you think about this topic, do an honest self-evaluation. Have you really tried everything you can to reach your goals? Are you willing to turn your obstacles into stepping stones?

Take a piece of paper and write your goal at the top. Then, below it, write three things you can do in the next week to get you closer to your goal.

Whatever you are working toward, whether it's weight loss, better health, or a business endeavor, the most important thing is that you never stop trying.

What other challenges did Erik Weihenmayer face on his journey? You can read his inspiring story in his book, *Touch the Top of the World: A Blind Man's Journey to Climb Farther than the Eye Can See: My Story*.

There were many smaller challenges before he made it to Everest. To meet his goals, Weihenmayer worked hard moving one step at a time.

No matter your challenge, keep looking for a way to overcome it. Never stop trying to make your life better. Success will come to those who refuse to quit.

Day 22 | Increase Your Knowledge to Conquer Your Mental Illness

K nowledge is power. No, really, it is.

You learn the lesson from your earliest days as an infant until the last day you draw breath.

As a baby, you first learn how crying makes your caregivers give you attention. Whether you're hungry, uncomfortable, or have a dirty diaper, letting out a good wail tells your guardians you have a need.

In time, we learn to ask for what we need, and the power of knowledge grows exponentially from there. Questions lead to answers and understanding.

When coping with a mental illness, knowledge is even more powerful. Your first bits of wisdom may come from a doctor or psychologist. Then your knowledge base grows to include friends, family, and helpful internet sites. Maybe you even first stumbled upon my writing and *Speaking Bipolar* in an attempt to gain understanding.

When an internist diagnosed me with Familial Mediterranean Fever, no one I knew had ever heard of the disease, including the internist. He stumbled upon it while researching my unexplained symptoms. Most everything I learned from then on has been based on my own research. Every time I meet a new doctor, I have to teach them about the rare condition.

Not to be overlooked is self-knowledge. To best cope with bipolar disorder, you have to keep track of the things that help you do better and the trends that make things worse.

When you have an illness, whether physical or mental, you have to be your own cheerleader. You have to advocate for yourself and insist on proper care from your doctors.

It's vital for you to take the initiative in caring for your health. No one will ever know you better than you know yourself. By taking the time to learn about your illness and the way it affects you, you learn to manage it more successfully.

For today, hunt for knowledge. You may choose to read through past journals or watch videos about your condition on YouTube. After you find helpful material, look for solutions to keep you moving forward.

Knowledge is power, so never stop seeking it.

Journal Prompt: What do you know now about taking care of yourself that you didn't know when first diagnosed? How does that wisdom help you?

Creative Writing Prompt: A young woman wakes up and suddenly knows everything. Write a story about how she uses her gift.

Explore the 4 Things a Chronic Illness Teaches You

Living every day with a chronic illness is not for wimps. This is a true statement, whether the illness is mental or physical. (Yes, bipolar disorder is a chronic illness.) An insidious evil enters your life and changes every day to follow.

Coping with illness is not a hopeless cause. Millions of people worldwide continue to live happy and productive lives, even with a chronic illness. They are able to do so because they understand the four lessons every chronic illness teaches you.

1. Looks Can Be Deceiving

CHRONIC ILLNESSES ARE often called invisible illnesses because they're not easily identifiable to outsiders. The person sitting next to you, with the bright smile, could be suffering from one of these ailments.

My life is full of a few ailments. The greatest two rivals, bipolar disorder and Familial Mediterranean Fever (FMF), limit my day-to-day life more than all the others combined.

Except for an occasional rash on the tops of my feet or lower legs, neither disease causes any outward signs. Unless you can tell from the black circles under my eyes or by the way I am dragging myself along, you would never know there is anything wrong with me.

The positive lesson here is knowing what I hide behind a smile has changed the way I look at other people. The person laughing the loudest may be the saddest. The man who surrounds himself with crowds of people may be the loneliest. The girl sitting quietly in the corner may be the funniest.

The only way to truly know someone is to take the time and effort to go below the surface. Everyone deserves this effort.

2. Flexibility Is Essential

MANY CHRONIC ILLNESSES create uncertainty in the patient's life. Someone who is feeling fine today may not be able to get out of bed tomorrow. Heck, the person leading the team in the morning may be incapable of movement come afternoon.

This uncertainty forces you to be flexible. You can try to fight against it. I know more than a few who try to stick to their prearranged plans no matter what, but the results are often disappointing.

People who are newly diagnosed are most likely to be inflexible. Part of learning to be flexible includes learning to accept your diagnosis. That acceptance may take months or years to achieve.

When you understand you have little control over tomorrow, it teaches you to be flexible. You may still get to go for a hike, but it may have to be a shorter one. Dinner out may still be an option, but you'll have to forego the movie afterwards. Going out late for a few drinks? Well, unfortunately, some things may not be possible. By being flexible, many things will be.

3. Success Involves Planning

IT MAY SEEM CONTRADICTORY for me to follow up talk of uncertainty with planning. I just said that you can't plan ahead, didn't I?

Yes and no.

While it's true you often have limited control over when a symptom starts, experience teaches you what things you can do to improve the odds.

One of my most frustrating health issues is gastroparesis, a partial paralysis of the lower portion of my stomach. Gastroparesis causes you to digest food very slowly, limiting how much you can eat during a meal.

After a few painful experiences, I learned to stay away from meat and other hard-to-digest foods before going places. If I do, chances are high I will be unable to go anywhere.

By learning how food and stress affect me, I know what and how much I can eat depending on what I want to do. For example, I go to Bible study one night during the week. To give myself the best chance of attending, the 12 hours before the meeting, I either don't eat or only have liquids. It may sound a little extreme, but most of the time it helps me go where I want.

The toughest thing for me is when I have to go places on several consecutive days. Skipping meals one day is fairly easy. Multiple days without solid food brings on a whole slew of additional problems. Yet, with proper planning, most of the time I can do what's needed.

Take note of patterns with your symptoms. What activities are harmless and which ones lead to increased trouble? Use those trends to help you plan ahead.

4. Bargains Are for More Than Shopping

IF YOU'VE HAD A CHRONIC illness for a while, you've probably heard of the spoon theory. First established online by Christine Miserandino over at But You Dont Look Sick[1], Christine compares the limited amount of energy you have with an illness to having a limited number of spoons. Every activity is only possible by spending or giving up a spoon.

1. http://butyoudontlooksick.com

Sometimes, just like with credit cards, you can overspend and use more spoons than you have. The price means that tomorrow you'll start the day with fewer spoons. Overdo today, pay the price tomorrow.

To learn to use my spoons in the best way, I bargain for the things that are most important to me. I can mow the lawn today OR I can go to Bible study tomorrow. Tonight I can go out with friends OR tomorrow I can work. Sometimes it feels like Sophie's Choice, but learning to bargain can make life more enjoyable.

Unfortunately, as illnesses progress, the number of spoons you start each day with tends to decrease. The new bargain may be more like choosing between spending today shopping *or* spending the next two days in bed. You may not be able to do everything, but by bargaining carefully, you should be able to do many things.

Learning these lessons quickly will help you live as full a life as possible. Yes, it sucks to have to say "no" to dinner plans because you have to go to the doctor tomorrow. And it hurts to stay home from a party because you know it's the only way you can make it to work tomorrow.

Try not to focus on what you are missing. Instead, each time you plan, bargain, or adapt successfully, celebrate the victory. A full life is possible, even with a chronic illness. The secret is to be strategic with the energy you have.

Day 23 | Learn from the Power of Redwood Seeds

When I was diagnosed with bipolar disorder in 1995, I thought my life was over. Many of my dreams felt like they were coming to a crashing end. I imagined I would never be more than a drooling zombie, disconnected from the world and the people I loved.

Accepting my mental illness and finding the right combination of medications to keep me stable was challenging, but I eventually got there. Yet, when I examined my life, it still felt like my biggest dreams could never happen.

I'm an extremely stubborn person and stick to my intentions like a barnacle on the side of a boat. It's a family trait that my mom says comes from our German ancestry. Whatever it is, when I put my mind to something, come hell or high water, I'm going to accomplish it.

Yet, when I came out of my bipolar stupor, I worried that even holding a job consistently would be impossible.

Still, I made a plan, and started to make small changes. Those tiny acts, such as forcing myself to bed at night and then up again when the alarm went off, each felt like meaningless actions, but each was a seed making future growth possible. I have worked 30-40 hours per week nearly every week since the end of 1995.

The power of seeds took root in other parts of my life as well. I started to write again and eventually started a blog. While *Speaking Bipolar* is hardly one of the most-known sites on the internet, it features hundreds of posts, over 300,000 words of content, and receives thousands of visitors each year. In addition, I've published hundreds of stories on *Medium, NewsBreak*, and other sites.

This book is a collection of articles that first appeared online, and I hope it will be the first book of many.

All of my writing production took time. I wrote each word one at a time, a few minutes every day for several years. Most of those writing and editing sessions felt like I was going nowhere, but now this book exists.

Conquering your bipolar disorder won't happen overnight, but every time you learn how to best cope with a part of it, you're planting a seed that will eventually grow into the life of your dreams.

Take a few minutes today to think about what you've already accomplished. If you are fighting an illness, what steps have you taken to understand and treat your condition? How has your treatment improved your life so far?

If you're one of the lucky, healthy individuals out there, think about another challenge in your life you need to overcome. What success have you achieved already? What small step can you take next?

You can fit about a dozen redwood seeds on a dime, but each of those seeds could grow to be a mighty tree, hundreds of feet tall. Every seed holds the power. What will you do with yours?

Journal Prompt: Where do you want to be in 10 years? Write a journal post as if you're already there and list the steps you took to get there. Then, pick one small seed, and start working toward your future goal.

Creative Writing Prompt: A talking bird drops an enchanted seed in your hand. Write a story about what happens when you plant it.

Take the Chance to Find Success

When you hear the quiet voice telling you to take a chance, you might picture a mischievous imp sitting on your shoulder. He's led you into trouble before, so you're unlikely to take his advice.

What if he's not wrong? Maybe taking the chance will open up the door to a fresh new world.

Wayne Gretzky is perhaps the most famous hockey player ever. Everyone, even non-hockey fans, knows his name. You'll often see his name on social media memes with words like, "You miss 100% of the shots you don't take."

In a simple statement, Gretzky reveals an important truth. You will never achieve success without taking a risk. True, you may fail. The risk might lead to disaster. Yet, the only way to succeed is to take the chance. You'll never score a goal if you don't take a shot.

The opportunities most missed are the tiny ones. You stop yourself from asking the girl behind the counter for her phone number because you fear rejection. You avoid applying for the job because you feel unqualified. Maybe you put off writing the story because you doubt readers will like it.

This happens with mental health, too. People refuse to seek treatment because they fear how medication will affect them. Men don't want to appear weak, so they don't talk about the struggles they are fighting inside. A mom is so busy caring for her family, she feels there's no time to address her anxiety and depression.

It's scary to take a chance. Rejection hurts. Unrealized dreams are painful, so to protect yourself, you choose inaction. In hockey terms, you put down your stick and walk away. But you might be leaving a glorious victory behind.

Would you know Wayne Gretzky's name if he had put down his hockey stick and quit playing?

Instead of thinking about how you might fail, concentrate on what would happen if you win. You never know which action will lead to success. Even if your first tries are unsuccessful, they may teach you what you need to know to reach your goal later.

An article you pound out on your keyboard in 20 minutes may resonate with millions of readers. The girl you ask out may become the love of your life. The job you felt inadequate for could be the career of your dreams. Talk therapy may help you make sense of the chaos in your mind and finally allow you to sleep at night.

The possibilities in life are endless. There are too many rags-to-riches stories for it to be impossible. Each tale includes someone who took a shot. Win or lose, they decided to try.

Your time might be now. The next shot could be your winning goal.

What risk scares you? Consider taking it today. Take the shot and see what you can achieve.

Day 24 | Celebrate Your Adaptability

I love trees. It's why they pop up often in my writing.

If you take the time to observe a tree, there's an abundance of lessons to learn. Trees are stalwart protectors, eternal givers, and vibrant artists.

One of my favorite traits is a tree's ability to be adaptable. Despite the hottest summers, the coldest winters, or the harshest windstorms, most trees survive. A few varieties stand fast for thousands of years.

Someone long ago named one of the oldest trees, Methuselah. They verified its age in 1957 as being at least 4,800 years old. Still listed as the oldest living tree on The Guinness World Records website, this tree knows the value of being adaptable. Imagine how much change that one tree has seen in just the last 100 years.

Side note: The Great Grandfather tree of Chile is thought to be over 5,000 years old, but there has been some disagreement on the age test.

Amazingly, humans are even more adaptable. If the COVID-19 pandemic taught you nothing else, you learned you can quickly adjust to a changed world. The process may be challenging, but you can adapt.

You're still here, walking your path, and taking in oxygen. That's proof of your adaptability. Better yet, you've already survived 100% of all the worst things thrown at you. With a 100% success ratio, nothing is impossible.

For today, think about the ways you've adapted to changing circumstances. Maybe it was a career change, a move to a faraway city, or the end of a long-term relationship. How did you learn to change? What did those lessons teach you?

You are better than a tree. Celebrate your adaptability. And if you get the chance, hug a tree. They supply much of our oxygen, after all.

Journal Prompt: What is the biggest challenge facing you today? How can you use the things you have learned in the past to help you adapt to this new situation?

Creative Writing Prompt: In a faraway land, trees talk. You visit the land to gain vital information. Write a story about the trip and what the trees tell you.

Make One Simple Change to Improve Your Life

Late one night, my sister reached out to me. She was watching a few of my video poems on the Speaking Bipolar YouTube channel and was concerned they were too dark. She reminded me I had stopped focusing on the positive.

To turn things around, she asked me to write a poem for her. She wanted a positive poem about a hope for the future. Over the next several days, *Dreams of Paradise* was born.

Writing this poem reminded me of a valuable lesson. Our mindset usually revolves around the things we are focusing on. When we focus on the negative, our whole life produces negative. However, if we focus on the positive, then good will follow.

Negative emotions often feel stronger. They seem to grip tighter and hold on longer. It takes little effort to stay in their darkness.

My poetry springs from my deepest parts, and there's a fair amount of pain there. Yet, not all the poetry I write is a perfect reflection of who I am. In fact, most of the time, I'm a positive person who loves to laugh and smile.

I have bipolar disorder and Familial Mediterranean Fever. The combination of the two gives me many opportunities to be negative. Most of the time, I choose not to be.

Yet, for a time, I was negative. All the time.

For years, my response whenever someone asked me how I was doing was to tell them, "I'm fine."

My mom gained a strange joy from following behind me and telling others that 'fine' never really meant fine. In fact, she told my friends that most of the time 'fine' meant terrible.

It's true; I was terrible. I was in constant pain and living with my worst enemy inside my head. It would be several years before the correct diagnosis of Familial Mediterranean Fever would reveal the physical pain I felt was real. Even so, I didn't want people to know I was terrible. I hate pity, so I wanted my pain to be my secret.

To change things, I started a new habit. At first, it was an attempt to be deceptive, to hide the truth from others. I decided I would smile no matter how I felt and tell everyone, "I'm good."

Who would think you're lying if you say you're good? It was a flawless plan. My new plan in place, I banished the word 'fine' from my vocabulary.

After a few weeks, there was an unexpected change. The more I told people I was good, and the more often I smiled and laughed, the more frequently it felt true. Life was full of more good things. My smiles and proclaimed goodness were making a difference.

No, my mental illness and physical pain didn't vanish. If only it were that simple. Rather, having a positive mindset changed the way it was affecting me. That simple change, just saying, "I'm good," made me notice more beauty in the world around me.

My sister's reminder to write a positive poem highlighted the importance of focusing on the good, and there is always some waiting to be found.

There are many reasons to be in a negative place. All you have to do is turn on the news for five minutes, and you sink to a darkness where surviving this life feels unlikely. Yet, there is still a lot of positive in the world.

Spring is my favorite season where I live in Southeast Tennessee. The leaves on the trees open and flowers of every color burst out of hiding. The extra time at home during the pandemic turned my yard into my sanctuary. Every time I work in the flower beds, I see the results of my hard work, and that goodness brings me pride and joy.

The world is full of sadness, and many of us don't have enough to meet our needs. Homelessness and hunger remain problems in a world full of abundance. Yet, even with such deprivations, there are still many reasons for gratitude.

For me, the green grass lining my yard, my cat's rhythmic purr, and the time I spend each day with my parents are all reasons for me to be grateful. I know my family loves me, and my faith is real. Meditating on the positives helps me conquer the toughest times.

My challenge to you is to do the same. Name three positive things in your life right now. It's easy to do. If you woke up in a home this morning, that's one. If you're breathing, that's two. You just need one more to have three for today.

When you look around you with eyes of gratitude, you'll quickly find much more than three things. Once you start your mind down the positive path, other useful things will come into view.

You may not have the power to change the world or fix your health, but you can change where you choose to focus. Decide to focus on the positive and watch how your life changes.

Day 25 | Embrace Every Failure

Why are we so afraid of failure? From our first days of school, we're taught that failing is the worst thing we can do, but failure is essential for growth.

Children learn to walk by repeatedly falling down. Each fall could be viewed as a failure, but the child doesn't quit. Imagine if a toddler made his first attempt to stand and fell back onto his plush diaper, devastated and unwilling to try again. We'd have billions of adults afraid to walk.

Kids are unstoppable. If they fall once or 100 times, they have an instinctual voice inside, pushing them to keep trying. The first steps may be wobbly and chaotic, but before long, they learn their stride, and then it's a race to keep up with them.

The fear of failure as adults often keeps you stuck where you are right now. Why not try to stand? The only way you'll know if you can walk is if you take a step.

Dealing with mental illness increases the desire to shut down after a failure. Each fall hurts, and the added weight of depression holds you down, but you shouldn't quit.

Just like your little girl learning to walk, you'll never know what you can do until you try. This might mean trying new medications, seeing a therapist or changing to a different one, exploring exercise options, or adopting healthier meal choices.

Having an illness should never keep you stuck. If what you're doing now isn't working, try something else. Fight until you learn to walk, and once you're there, learn another skill. In time, you may learn to fly.

Take a few minutes today to explore the options in front of you. If you're not sure what to do next, reach out to a friend who can help or find a community online. Like-minded souls can help you see options you've never considered.

Sitting on the floor accomplishes nothing, so dare to fail. Get up and see what you can achieve.

Journal Prompt: When did you keep going after a perceived failure? How did you do it? Can that life lesson help with today's problems?

Creative Writing Prompt: Write a story about someone who has an epic failure that leads them to their greatest success.

Believe It's Okay to Be a Disaster

Your mental health may be a mess, chaotic, or even a disaster. That's okay. Stop beating yourself up. It's been said that every master was once a disaster.

We often think of inspirational quotes as fuel for achieving goals. Those goals might include starting a business, writing a book, or training for a marathon. However, achieving balanced and stable mental health is just as essential of a goal.

Most days, I'm still a disaster. I like to write about the positive things in life, but things on the inside are often dark and scary. My love life was so messy that I stopped dating altogether. That's a story best told in another book.

My work life isn't much better. For decades, I've bounced from job to job, rarely staying anywhere longer than three years.

The dial on my bathroom scale spins up and down like a yo-yo. And my mental health? It may be relatively stable, but it's far from ideal. Nearly 30 years into my bipolar journey, there are still days I can't get out of bed or am afraid to leave the house.

I'm still a disaster. But you know what? That's okay.

Look at anyone successful in history and, before their success, you'll see plenty of disasters. Thomas Edison tried thousands of ideas before he created the light bulb. The Wright Brothers failed with a printing business before turning to flight, and then it took dozens of launches before they finally got a vessel into the air.

Every success is built on a foundation of failures. Usually lots of them.

The early days of my journey to control my bipolar disorder are a line of disasters. From the time I was committed to a psychiatric hospital until I finally felt in control of my life again took a few years. I started and stopped 30 different medications during that time, and some were epic failures. I fought everything from migraines to suicidal mania as my care team and I worked to find the right drug cocktail for my brain chemistry.

In addition, there were four therapists, three psychiatrists, two periods where I couldn't work at all, and a partridge in a pear tree. Okay, so maybe not the last one, but you get the picture.

It was a very rough time for me. I'd be lying if I didn't say I thought about ending it every single day. Most of those years, I felt survival was impossible. Success with bipolar felt like an unattainable dream, a mirage I would never reach.

Yet, I kept fighting. A tiny voice in my head told me, if I could survive each disaster, I would eventually reach my goal. And I was right.

Not only did I learn to live successfully with mental illness, I also discovered I had a physical chronic illness and how to cope with it. Those lessons enabled me to help others face similar challenges.

Living with illness often means our disasters are out of our control. When we go to bed at night, everything may be okay. The next morning may greet us with a very different world.

Those new and unexpected disasters can devastate you, making you feel like giving up. They can also teach you something.

While sometimes health disasters come out of the blue with seemingly no trigger, most of the time you can see a trend or an event that caused things to get worse.

- Maybe you did too much when you needed to rest.

- Maybe you had too much alcohol when you knew it would negatively affect your medication.

- Maybe you spent time around emotional vampires.

Whatever caused the disaster, there's usually something you can learn from it. As you learn from each rough patch, the knowledge will help you move forward toward becoming a master.

Each disaster you survive teaches you how strong you can be. At the moment, you may feel like there's no way out, but there always is. It's a matter of holding on to hope and pushing forward. It means recognizing that, while today you may not have the strength to take a shower and get dressed, tomorrow you might.

Even if tomorrow is bad, there will be a day soon when things will be better. I'm not saying things will go from awful to great, but they will be better than where you are right now.

Are you a disaster? Great! Welcome to the club. You will probably be here again, and I'll be here to welcome you. Being a disaster can be painful, but it's not fatal. If you refuse to give up, better days will come.

Celebrate your disasterhood. Own it and acknowledge it. Be the best disaster you can be.

You may not be a master today, but chances are good you won't be a disaster tomorrow.

Day 26 | Stay Positive When Life Throws You a Curveball

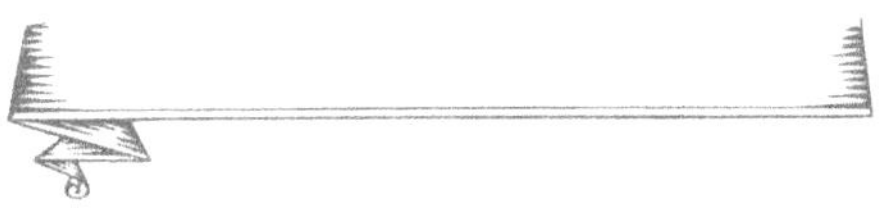

Life is full of curveballs. Even the best plans sometimes come to nothing. Does that mean you should stop trying? Of course not.

When you receive a chronic or mental illness diagnosis, it can feel like your world is knocked off its axis. Suddenly, you're being redirected down roads you never knew existed. And at times, it's terrifying.

Before I received my Familial Mediterranean Fever diagnosis, I went through months of medical tests. After one, where I ate radioactive eggs and then had a technician track their progress through my body, another curveball smacked me in the head. A few days later, a nurse called to tell me I had gastroparesis. Yet another box on my chronic illness bingo card received its dab.

The nurse told me I could never again eat fresh fruits and vegetables, meat, or nuts. The news was crushing. Food is one of my greatest pleasures, but what the nurse said was an exaggeration.

On top of all I was already juggling with my bipolar disorder, I now had a new curveball: gastroparesis. In a nutshell, gastroparesis is a paralysis of the stomach, particularly the bottom part. Your lower stomach is supposed to churn and grind up the food you eat so it can pass into your intestines. As the stomach becomes paralyzed, the churning slows or stops, and food stays in your stomach, causing bloating, pain, and nausea.

The curveball came out of the blue but led to dozens of new recipes. The fresh recipes introduced me to dozens of flavors I'd never sampled before. I learned what I could eat and when it was safe. The way I ate changed to a slower, more deliberate pace, and the times I ate also changed. Now, I savor each bite with mindfulness, chewing longer to grind up every morsel.

Despite what the nurse told me, gastroparesis wasn't the end of my food journey. Instead, it was a curveball, a detour that forced me to change.

There is a wonderful aspect to literal detours. When you're forced to drive down a road you've never been on before, you'll often see amazing sights. Maybe you'll find a beautiful old building hidden in a forgotten area of your town. Maybe the detour will give you a glimpse of the sunset in a breathtakingly unique setting. Detours can also expose you to wildlife you might not otherwise see.

These are only road detours. Exploring detours in life can be just as beautiful.

You never know what you can do until you face a situation where you have to do it. I never imagined I could work full time with both a mental and chronic illness, but yet I do it every day. My curveballs taught me what I can do. They showed me how a full life is possible no matter how many balls are hurled at your head. Every course change taught me that what matters is how you choose to face the disruption.

Life will toss you changes without any warning, but how you handle them is in your power. Choose to find a positive way through and the curveball will help you grow.

Journal Prompt: What's the biggest curveball ever thrown at you? How did you adapt to the changes? What did it teach you?

Creative Writing Prompt: Driving to work one day, your character is forced to take a detour. Distracted, they make a wrong turn and end up in an enchanted world. Write a story about what happens next.

Start A Gratitude Jar

Gratitude is a gift. It brings you joy on the good days, and hope on the harder days.

Gratitude breeds contentment, which leads to a happier life. It keeps your heart positive and optimistic.

As wonderful as the above sounds, being grateful can be difficult. A day of bipolar depression or intense pain caused by a chronic illness can push gratitude far from your mind.

I understand. I have bipolar disorder, generalized anxiety disorder, and Familial Mediterranean Fever, just to name my worst foes. There are others, too. If one thing isn't beating me down, then another one is taking its turn.

In this chapter, you will learn about gratitude jars. You'll learn why you should have a gratitude jar and how to start one.

Staying positive is a challenge when you are coping with mental illness. While an attitude of gratitude is internal, a gratitude jar is something external you can see when you need a boost.

Dark days with bipolar disorder block most light from your world. It's too easy to spiral further into the darkness. Imagining reasons to be grateful can feel impossible.

When you have something tangible to look at, it reminds you there are many blessings in your life. Those gifts make the tough days easier to handle.

There are three principal ways gratitude can help you.

The first way a gratitude jar can help is to give you inner peace. Focusing on the negative steals your internal calm. If you only think about what's missing, you stop seeing what's in front of you.

Remembering what you have and the people who love you gives you back your peace. Gratitude focuses your mind on contentment. A content mind is less anxious.

The second benefit is hope. Coping with depression can make you feel hopeless. Everything goes dark. You may fear it will never get better.

By keeping a gratitude jar in sight, you can see reasons for hope. Even if you don't open the jar, seeing those bits of paper with your handwritten notes will remind you of the good in your life.

Hope is essential for dealing with mental illness. Keeping a gratitude jar puts your reasons for hope in front of you.

The third way a gratitude jar is beneficial is that it promotes positivity.

Pain, nausea, racing thoughts, severe depression–living with bipolar gives you many reasons to be negative. As your illness disrupts your life, things may grow bleak.

On those days, it's time to open your gratitude jar and take out some of those notes. On each one, you'll find a message with a reason to think of good things. Those reasons for being thankful don't disappear simply because today is a bad day.

Now that you know about the benefits of having a gratitude jar, here's how to start one.

Want to hear something great? A gratitude jar doesn't have to cost you a penny. However, if you want to buy a special jar for this purpose, that's always an option.

You'll want to pick a clear jar. An old peanut butter or pickle jar will work just fine. My current jar is a pasta canister.

To dress up your jar, add stickers, ribbon, or glitter. It's your jar, so do what you like.

The type of jar doesn't matter, but it's important you can see what's in it even when it's on the shelf. On those hard days when you're stuck in bed or lounging on the sofa, you'll want to see your jar and how many slips of paper are in it.

Once you have your jar, it's time to add to it. You can use sticky notes or any scrap of paper. Make it your goal to add three slips of paper to your jar every day.

Did someone make you smile today? Write their name on a piece of paper. Was your dinner tasty? Write that down. Do you have a comfortable bed or a cozy blanket? That's another reason.

Anything that adds joy or comfort to your life is a reason to be grateful. Write it down.

Some days are tougher than others, but even those days have reasons to be grateful. You just need to look harder.

The next time dark days hit you, remember your gratitude jar. Keep it within sight so you can always see how many reasons you have to be thankful.

When things get especially dark, open your jar and pull out some of your notes. Let your words encourage you and remind you of what's important. Use those messages to pick yourself up again so you can hold on to hope.

Gratitude is a gift. Choosing to focus on your blessings makes it easier to cope with the rough days of living with illness.

Day 27 | Feel Your Emotions and Let the Tears Fall

Every week, I post fresh stories and inspirational quotes to promote positivity.

As vital as positivity is to good mental health, this chapter is about crying. You may wonder what crying has to do with positivity, but crying can be a positive thing. Our bodies were designed to cry, both to express emotion and to release toxins.

Many people don't like to cry. Personally, I'll do everything I can to stop up my tear ducts, but I know it's an important thing to do from time to time.

The best crying comes after a body-shaking laugh with your closest friends. You remember those happy tears for years.

I remember a time decades ago when six of us were gathered around a dining room table playing cards. We laughed a lot. One friend laughed so hard she peed her pants. The more she laughed, the more she peed, and the more we all laughed until we couldn't breathe. It was the best of times.

Talk about a dramatic interruption to a game of Euchre. The people in the next room never understood, and we chose to keep the joke a secret.

Then there's the type of crying that comes from loss. Losing your soulmate or child brings on the most painful tears. Your heart breaks as each drop of water meanders down your face.

The value of crying is in owning your emotions. You must accept how you feel before you can move forward. Accepting your feelings includes letting yourself experience them. Feel the joy. Embrace the sadness.

Mental illness teaches you to hide your emotions, even from yourself. Those feelings serve a purpose, and bottling them up only leads to more pain.

If you need to laugh, laugh until no more air comes. If you need to cry, then cry until your eyes run dry. Let yourself feel every emotion so you can move forward again.

Part of dealing with a mental illness is grieving the life you wished for yourself. It's okay to cry during your grieving process. Some of those tears might come back year after year, so let them fall and feel all your feels. Grief has no time limit, and that's true even if you're grieving a life you will never experience.

Tears that last too long can be a sign of a bigger problem. If you cry uncontrollably or for days on end, it's time to talk to your mental health care provider. However, occasional tears are healthy.

For today, give yourself permission to cry. Find a sad movie online and let it pull at your heartstrings until the tears fall. *Little Women*, *The Hours*, and *Moulin Rouge* are a few movies that elicit my tears. Ewan McGregor's howl at the end of *Moulin Rouge* rips my soul out.

If you don't need sad tears, call your best friend who always makes you laugh. Take them to lunch or schedule a phone date. Let them tell you funny stories until your face is crusty from the salt of your tears. If they're not available, the TV show, *Friends*, always makes me laugh. *How I Met Your Mother* and *The Big Bang Theory* are two other great comedies.

Crying is a beautiful gift, even if it doesn't always feel like it. It's also an essential part of managing your mental health.

Let your tears fall.

Journal Prompt: What were your happiest tears? Describe the day and how you felt.

Creative Writing Prompt: Write a story about a world with no tears. Why does no one cry?

Remember the Immeasurable Value of the Little Things

When I was in the 8th grade, a new girl moved into my school and into my life. Heather was a quiet, plain-looking girl—the kind you could easily overlook.

It's a sad fact that most of us didn't see her. At least, not the real her.

One day during lunch period, Heather walked up and asked for my help. I don't remember what she needed, but I excused myself to go sit alone with her at another table. For a few minutes, she had my full attention.

I didn't know how tough it was for her to ask for help. Later, I learned how painfully shy she was and the dark reasons she kept to herself.

Those few minutes with Heather meant nothing to me. Had it not been for the following, I would have completely forgotten the event. My only sacrifice was missing a few minutes of gossiping with friends while munching on smoked almonds.

To Heather, those few moments touched her heart. She felt my willingness to give her my time—an uncommon kindness in her life—was the greatest gift in the world.

To show her gratitude, Heather wrote me a note and included the words to the Mary Dawson Hughes poem, *The Little Things*.

It starts:

It really is the little things

That mean the most of all...
The "let me help you with that" things
That may seem very small...
– Mary Dawson Hughes

While I'll never remember what I did for Heather, I'll never forget receiving her note and how it made me feel. I realized how little I noticed her value and promised myself I would be better.

Sadly, Heather wasn't in my life for long. Months later, she moved away, and shortly after she died in a car accident.

I carried Heather's handwritten note in my wallet for years. It reminded me how even the simplest things can touch someone's life. We just need to do something.

Pick a flower and give it to a friend. Open a door for a stranger. Send a meaningful text message. Offer your time. Smile.

Those tiny acts of kindness have the power to change someone's day. We never know when the simplest act will have the greatest impact.

Make it your aim to be kind and generous with your time.

I can never repay Heather for the lesson she taught me. Instead, I live each day looking for the next Heather I can help.

Find your Heather and give the gift of yourself.

Day 28 | Never Give up on Your Dreams

While I was going up, I dreamed of being a writer. In my fantasies, I imagined one day I would live in a cozy cabin on the side of a mountain overlooking a sprawling lake. Most days, I would sit close to my steaming cup of coffee, a thick cardigan wrapped around me, and the words would seep effortlessly from my mind.

Around age nine, I started writing on bits of paper. Carefully folded and stapled, I perfected my handwriting and wrote tiny books. Yet I dreamed of more.

My dad decided I could use an old manual typewriter. I plunked away on those heavy keys until the ribbon left only a faint hint of ink behind. Noticing my determination, my father upgraded me to his electric typewriter.

I was the king of the world, and my publishing empire was taking off. The sound of the typewriter's low hum filled me with glee, and I typed as often as I could.

All of my free time went into creating a family newsletter, typed with great care on five-part paper. Carbon paper transferred the imprint from page to page. *The Informer* was my first newsletter, produced long before I would ever hear of the internet.

My dream was coming true, and nothing could stop it. Except, in time, I put it on hold. I got busy living life.

I was a social teenager, and my need for interaction slowly pushed my writing out of the picture.

I grew and changed, eventually leaving Wisconsin and moving to Tennessee when I was 20. I wasn't writing, but I was on my way. There would always be time for writing.

At 23, a doctor in a psychiatric hospital diagnosed me with bipolar disorder. As I spent hazy days confined within the walls of the treatment center, my mind occasionally drifted off to writing. I vowed to write again, but never seriously pursued it until 10 years later.

Life in the world had changed me, and while my dream was to be famous for my fiction works, it became increasingly essential for me to share my struggles with mental illness. Since 2018, I've been writing extensively online, publishing hundreds of thousands of words of content.

An internet search for Scott Ninneman will pull up dozens of my stories on various sites. This is the first book with my name on the cover, and hopefully, the first of many.

Even though life became more challenging with my illnesses, my dream is alive. That you are now holding this book in your hands is proof that dreams can come true, even if you have a mental illness.

Your dreams don't end because you received a painful diagnosis. It may take more steps to reach your goal, but anything is possible.

Give your dreams wings and let them take flight.

Spend some time today thinking about your dreams. Are there goals you set aside because life got in the way? Dust off those visions of your potential future and take the first steps toward reaching your prize.

Journal Prompt: What was your biggest dream as a child? Did you achieve it? Is it a goal you can work toward now? What would be the first step?

Creative Writing Prompt: Write a story about a child who grows up in one night and wakes up to their dream come true.

Help Others by Being One Step Ahead

I am no personal development guru, nor have I mastered anything in this life. My biggest skill is watching TV, but you hardly get awards for that. I'm also a great listener, but a lot of that is me fighting in my head over what to say next. The awkward silence encourages the other person to keep talking.

You may wonder why I write about self-improvement. The answer is simple. Helping others is not about being an expert.

Don't panic. That's the truth. All the gurus out there have been lying to you for years. You don't need an expert for most things.

While I don't have every answer, I have kept myself alive for over 50 years. That feat is worthy of an award when you factor in my bipolar disorder and other chronic illnesses.

My decades of trudging along on this earth taught me a thing or two. Those lessons can help others. So, I write them down. You have useful knowledge, too.

As an introvert, I struggle to be around people. Yet, I love to teach. I am nothing but a bowl full of contradictions.

It's a special moment when the person you are training fully understands your lesson. When they realize they can repeat the process, you, as a teacher, get a special warm and fuzzy feeling. Once upon a time, I wanted to be a schoolteacher. While that goal didn't pan out, there are still things I can teach.

My goal now is to write to help others. The beautiful thing about helping others is that you don't have to be an expert. No, instead, you only have to be a little further along than the person you're assisting.

Let's take hiking as an example. When I was healthier, I loved to hike. When you're a mile into rugged landscape, you're bound to find a stream or gully you have to cross.

Imagine you're with a small group of hikers and come to a creek you've never crossed before. After reviewing the possibilities, one person takes the lead and begins to find a path forward.

With each step, the other hikers pay close attention to the leader. They notice when a rock is unstable, or a spot is slippery. By watching, they learn where they should step next. The leader may even point to a rock and tell them, "Be sure you don't step here."

Has the leader suddenly become a hiking expert? Certainly not. However, the insight they gain from being the first one across makes them a valuable asset for those to follow. They may not know everything about hiking, but the new knowledge they've gained is of use to others.

We're all proverbial hikers. We may not be on the same path or moving in the same direction at the same time, but we're all wandering through this world.

As we make our journeys, there are many creeks and gullies to cross. Each time we successfully navigate an obstacle, it gives us valuable knowledge we can share with others.

My hiking days are limited now, but I have other lessons I can share. Those experiences keep me writing even though I'm a master of nothing.

You, too, are full of wisdom others need. You may have gotten married, divorced, lost a loved one, had children, quit a job, moved to a different country, and whatever else. Each experience gives you insights that could benefit others.

At the start of this chapter, you may have thought you never succeeded at anything. While that's not true, this story isn't about arguing with your negative self-talk. Whether you've succeeded or failed isn't important today. Why not?

Because your failures have value.

Let's go back to our hiking group. If the leader of the pack stepped on a slippery rock and plunged into the stream, you might consider their fall as a failure. Yet, watching them tumble teaches you to avoid the treacherous stone.

Other failures in life can be just as valuable to those behind us.

Were you fired from a job? You can teach others to be better employees with the knowledge of what you did wrong. Did you ruin a relationship? The power of hindsight shared with a friend can help strengthen their relationship. Were you a teen prone to poor choices? Telling younger ones where you slipped up can help them make better choices.

Each time you fail, you gain valuable insight. That value is something that can and should be shared.

I've failed a lot, and it's why I have so many lessons in my head.

Every step you take can teach those who will come after you. It doesn't matter if you've climbed Mount Everest or a local ant hill. Your greatest expertise in this moment might be just knowing which rock to avoid.

Someone crossing a stream doesn't care about how to get to the top of the mountain unless they are nearly there. Instead, they need to know where to place their foot right now. Is that next log safe to step on? If you know, you can help.

In a sense, you are a master. Your experiences taught you lessons others don't know. There is at least one person on a similar journey right behind you. The only difference between your journeys is that you are a little farther along.

Be generous and take the time to share your wisdom with those following you. You'll both be glad you did.

Day 29 | Persevere Like a Cuckoo Clock

I love mechanical clocks. The more intricate and complicated, the better. From grandfather clocks to cuckoos, they all amaze me. Once upon a time, I even dreamed of designing cuckoo clocks.

We had a cuckoo in my childhood home, and it still hangs on the wall in my parent's house. It was old when I was a kid, but now it's got another 50 years under its belt.

It amazed me how a series of two pinecone-shaped weights could keep the clock running and the cuckoo singing.

Later, I learned of other amazing clocks with dancing characters and stirring music. The famous Glockenspiel in the New City Hall on Marienplatz in Munich is one such clock. Though never fully automatic, it's amazing what the clockmaker accomplished. His masterpiece still runs over 100 years later.

It makes me sad how digital clocks have eliminated the desire to build mechanical masterpieces, but the lesson for today is to learn from what clocks do.

My parent's cuckoo clock is an 8-day clock. If I pull the weights to the top, the clock will run for eight days without needing further attention. Day or night, for decades, it's ticked away the seconds of our lives.

Like our old timekeeper, you have to do the same. Keep doing your job and move forward. Hard days will come. There will be days when you have to hide in bed or surf the sofa for an entire weekend, but the rest of the time, you need to keep going.

Look at a clock and remember this lesson every time you feel like quitting.

Journal Prompt: Look around your home. What's another object that can teach you a life lesson? What is the lesson?

Creative Writing Prompt: Imagine the characters in the famous Glockenspiel were real people placed there by a curse. Immovable, they watched everything during the last hundred years. Write a story about one of them.

Examine a Life Lesson Learned From My Uncle's Silence

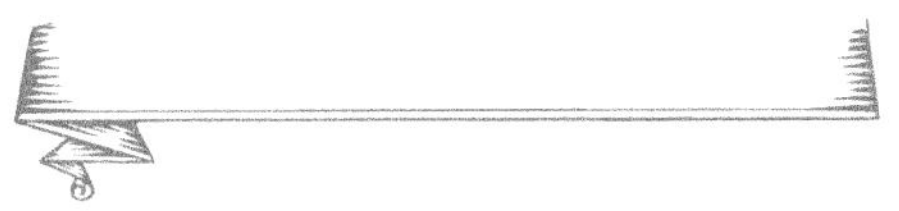

Not long ago, my uncle passed away. He died quietly alone in a nursing home where he had been confined the last few months of his life. My family lives many miles away, so it was a full day before we heard the sad news.

My knowledge of my uncle is limited. He didn't like children, and he was a quiet man with an aversion to small talk. Still, in his passing, I've learned an important life lesson.

My uncle was a veteran and served two tours in Vietnam. My mom, his sister, says he came back from war a different person, someone she never again recognized. The brother she knew died at war. The new person is the one he stayed for the rest of his life.

My heart broke as I watched my mother grieve for her younger brother. However, even more painful was the loss of potential and the relationships that could have been.

In the years I was growing up, I only remember my uncle speaking to me one time. 'Speaking' may not be the right term because he was yelling.

My uncle lived two doors down from my grandmother. My young cousins and I loved to play at my grandmother's house. She usually preferred we play outside.

During a day of play, we would run back and forth between grandma's and my uncle's house. Sometimes we played tag or follow the leader, and other times we ran the path just because the house in between had a covered walkway that was fun to run through.

At times, we ran the distance just to see my uncle's dog because of his funny name: Pooper. Pooper was an old pit bull, and, like my uncle, he disliked kids. I'm sure our running and laughing tormented the old dog confined by a short, heavy metal chain. He barked and snarled as we ran past just beyond his reach, his fierceness expressing his annoyance.

Our game of making Pooper bark and run back and forth in his confined space drove my uncle to the breaking point. He charged out from where he was repairing an engine in his garage, his face red with anger. Uncle screamed and cursed us with vicious words we rarely heard as children. Terrified of what he might do, we ran away and never teased Pooper again.

In the 20 years that I lived in the same town as my uncle, that's the only time I ever remember him talking directly to me. A dozen angry words. Even when his mother died, I'm sure he must have been at the funeral, but I have no memory of him speaking a single word to anyone.

A few days after his death, I found a copy of my uncle's obituary online. It shook me to my core to realize how little I knew about a blood relative.

I knew my uncle served in Vietnam. My aunt and grandmother reminded us often of how the war made him gruff and isolated. What I didn't know was how long he had been in Vietnam or how many medals he had received for his service.

I'm embarrassed to say that I had no clue where my uncle worked for the last 30 years of his career. I never met his second wife or any of her children, and I only have faint images of his first wife. Once he was gone, there was nothing I could do to fix any of those deficiencies.

Various people touch our lives every day. Thinking of my uncle caused me to stand still in the grocery store one afternoon. I was in the store for roughly 45 minutes. During that time, I nodded and smiled at dozens of people. I only spoke to one of them and our conversation lasted just a few seconds.

Grocery shopping is one of my least favorite activities. I approach the store like a man on a mission. List in hand, I map the quickest route through the store with the goal of getting in and out as quickly as possible.

I live in a small town with exactly three traffic lights. Most of the last two decades, I worked in fields that put me face to face with many of my fellow citizens. It's common for me to run into a dozen people I know when I just want a bag of potato chips so I can go home. As an introvert, all the interaction is overwhelming, so I race through my task.

On that afternoon, I was standing in line waiting for the self-service registers—you know, the counters where you can get your food and leave the store without talking to anyone. Scanning the crowd, I thought of my uncle.

As I surveyed the people within my viewing range, I thought about how I knew nothing about most of them. I didn't know their history or stories or even their names. Yet, each one had a tale that should be told.

For whatever reason, my uncle couldn't share his stories. Maybe he just didn't want to, or thinking of the past was too painful for him. I'll never know.

My mom told me he never talked about any of his war experiences. We know he lost close friends, but we know little more about his tour of duty. The stories he could have shared are now gone forever.

Would it have been worth my time to try to get to know my uncle? Could I have learned more about him if I tried? Is there anything I could have done to help him open up and tell his stories?

I'll never know the answer to those questions. My uncle sleeps now, and that door of opportunity is closed for good.

As I traverse my 50s, I'm becoming more of a loner and a homebody. My days of solitude help me relate to the life my uncle lived.

I could easily be the man charging out of my house to yell at children running nearby. I don't, but I could see how it could happen.

With his silence, my uncle taught me a life lesson. My life isn't over, and I have a lot of stories yet to be told. I'm not a soldier, and I never served in a war, but I have fought many battles. Maybe those stories will be useless to many, but maybe there's one person who could benefit.

My recommendation is to share your stories. Whether you're a writer putting words on paper or a campfire storyteller, stop keeping your stories to yourself. Those words are your history and no one else can tell it.

My uncle had a library in his head, hundreds of stories left untold. Like the library of Alexandria, his library is gone forever.

Whether you are ten or a hundred or anywhere in between, you have stories. There's a library of tales living in your head, stories of heroic acts and tales of painful loss. Deep inside, you hold words of internal turmoil and the wisdom that helped you survive. Those stories need to be told.

As brave as my uncle was, he didn't feel strong enough to share his stories. I know he was stronger than he realized, but I didn't tell him when I had the chance. Instead, I'm here sharing his story with you. Hopefully, his silence will teach you to be brave enough to share your past.

Tell your stories. Share your truth. Dispense your wisdom. The world needs what you have to tell. You are the only one who can tell your stories.

Day 30 | Celebrate Every Win, No Matter How Small

When was your last win? Yesterday? A month ago? When you were 12? I'll bet it was today, but you may not have even noticed.

As busy humans, we get so fixed on our big goals that we lose sight of what we're accomplishing along the way. But every big win is made up of dozens of smaller ones.

No one gets up one morning and runs a marathon with no training and imagines they will win. To reach the finish line, you run every day. Frosty mornings and rainstorms don't stop you. Instead, you get your butt out of bed and lace up your shoes. Every time you go out the door, it's a win. You should celebrate every mile you cross. The tiny wins push you toward the bigger ones.

You don't cross the finish line every day. Significant milestones may be days, weeks, or even years apart. Most days are about training. You spend your time working to get closer to the next goal.

It would be wonderful if every day included a major win, a golden trophy symbolizing success, but all the other days are just as important.

"But, Scott," you may be thinking. "I'm not a runner. I'm barely a walker."

Me too.

When you have a mental illness, victory often feels impossible. Weeks can go by where surviving seems hopeless. Simple tasks, such as getting out of bed or washing your hair, may require monumental effort. I get it. I struggle through those awful days, too. Those days suck, but no matter how bad you feel, you are still winning.

After battling bipolar for decades, every day still has its obstacles. Mental illness brings its own version of thunderstorms and frigid winds. To conquer it, we never stop training.

Every time you take your meds, eat healthy food, or force yourself to bed when you'd rather binge-watch the next five episodes of *Grey's Anatomy*, you're training. When you write in your journal, practice gratitude, or skip coffee after lunch because you know what it does to your sleep pattern, you're winning.

Celebrate the victory.

Some days, the only success is staying alive, but that counts, too. I know how hard it can be. Acknowledge your win.

Never forget how much every day matters. Living with bipolar disorder is a marathon, so keep training. What you do today affects all your tomorrows. Practice healthy habits now and it will make your future days easier to face.

So, I ask again, when was your last win? Celebrate your victory.

Journal Prompt: What was your biggest win? How did it make you feel? What did it teach you?

Creative Writing Prompt: Your character is the underdog in a race. There's no chance they can win, but they are determined to compete. Write a story about the race from their perspective.

Believe You Are Successful

Impostor syndrome. It's one of the buzz phrases of our time.

The idea is hardly something new. People have always had insecurities, but the way we talk about it today has changed. Many of us believe we are somehow less than because we feel insecure.

Like most people, impostor syndrome is frequently on my mind. I'm constantly asking myself, "Do I give my family all they deserve? Is my work of high quality? Am I a successful adult? Is my writing any good?"

One day while scrolling through *Medium*, a story with similar questions grabbed my attention. As I read the author's words, I marveled at how it felt like they were pulled straight out of my head. The writer said she was middle-aged and still not sure what she wanted to do with her life.

Yeah, me too, I thought.

Later that day, I mentioned the story to my mom and shared how I still didn't feel grown up. She was in her late-70s at the time and told me how she still felt the same way. I wondered if the two of us and the *Medium* writer were the only three people in the world who felt that way.

All the online talk about internal insecurities made me wonder, does anyone really have it all together? Is there anyone who genuinely feels successful? What about the leaders in business or best-selling authors? How do the influencers with millions of followers feel?

It's easy to look at successful individuals like Oprah Winfrey or James Patterson and think, "If anyone feels secure in themselves, it has to be them." But, do they really? In the middle of the night, when those troubling insecurities come calling, what do they think about? Do they question whether they'll ever get it together?

I don't know Oprah or Patterson, but based on my human experience, I imagine they feel like the rest of us. They may be less likely to own up to it, but the feelings are still there.

One of my closest friends was in her mid-90s when we lost her. She was full of wisdom and life lessons. I never left her house disappointed that I'd taken the time to visit her.

When we were together, we laughed about all the silliness in the world. We reminisced about our favorite memories and reflected on friends no longer with us. She told me about the world that existed decades before I came to be, and I shared stories of today's woes of social media and technology.

It never failed, at some point in our conversation, we always talked of things we were working to improve. Though she was legally blind, she read daily using audiobooks. She used her time and limited energy to better herself.

After nearly a century of life, she told me one day, "I don't think I'll ever get it all together."

Yep, sweetheart, you're not alone.

So, what do you do about imposter syndrome? If none of us feels like we know what we're doing, then the only option is to keep going. Learn what you can. Practice your art. Keep showing up and growing.

If we will never overcome impostor syndrome, let's stop thinking about it. Let's have the attitude, "I don't know what I'm doing, but I'm going to keep doing it, anyway."

After all, what's the other option? To do nothing? No, of course not. Life has to go on, and so must we.

There will be days you feel like you're getting it all wrong. You may feel you have no clue what you're doing. But, you know what? You're doing it. Even better, you're teaching others as they see you keep going.

Do you feel like an impostor? Congratulations! You're a human. Own it. Accept it. Then get back to moving forward. Stumble if you have to, but never stop trying to improve.

Who knows, maybe someday you'll feel like you've figured it out. Maybe you will wake up one morning and know you are a good parent, writer, or employee.

More likely, imposter syndrome will stick with you, keeping doubt in the back of your mind for as long as you breathe oxygen. If that's the case, then try to at least have some fun along the way.

Explore What's Next

Congratulations! You've reached the end of the first *30 Days of Positivity* book. Your journey is endless, though, and I have the perfect tools to help you stay on the positive path.

Every week, I publish two newsletters. The Sunday *All Things Bipolar Newsletter*[1] includes the freshest content about bipolar life. The *Speaking Bipolar Positivity Club*[2] has weekly posts following a similar format to the chapters in this book. Both newsletters will help you better understand mental illness so you can live your best life.

You can also find me as "Speaking Bipolar" on most social media sites.

We are all endless works-in-progress. With the tiniest bit of effort, you can continue to improve every day. Think about how far you've come in the last 30 days and then imagine what else is possible.

Staying positive in this world is tough. I hope the chapters of this book have helped you remember there is good in your life. You are part of that good, and you have the power to make your life better than it's been.

Keep looking for the positive in your life. Feel your emotions and share your love. One day at a time, you can help change the world.

What's next is up to you, but I hope you'll decide to keep moving forward. Your world is what you make it, so choose carefully.

Until next time, keep fighting.

---

1. *https://speakingbipolar.com/newsletter*

2. *https://speakingbipolar.com/club*

SCOTT NINNEMAN

Scott Ninneman

Don't miss out!

Visit the website below and you can sign up to receive emails whenever Scott Ninneman publishes a new book. There's no charge and no obligation.

https://books2read.com/r/B-A-NQWTB-KNHRD

BOOKS 2 READ

Connecting independent readers to independent writers.

About the Author

Scott Ninneman loves to help people find the positive in this chaotic world.

Diagnosed with both bipolar 1 disorder and generalized anxiety disorder, mental health is both his life and his passion. Scott believes words can heal, and hopes his content will give you the strength you need to keep going.

Scott is a quiet country boy living in the mountains of southeast Tennessee. He spends his days rearranging numbers while working as a bookkeeper and tax preparer. In his free time, Scott volunteers, cares for his mother, and creates lots of online content for his Speaking Bipolar blog, Medium, Substack, and NewsBreak. He loves working in his yard, hiking, cooking, and watching science-fiction series.

You can find hundreds of his articles on the web. Besides writing about bipolar, Scott shares stories about self-improvement, living with chronic illness, caregiving, and poetry.

Life may not be what you had hoped it would be, but it's still worth living. You can live a full life with mental illness, and Scott wants to help you do it.

Until next time, keep fighting.

Read more at https://speakingbipolar.com.